Jeff & M...

Thanks for being
a special part of
our lives through
so many years!

May my book be
uplifting to you
both! Love,
Kristi
October 2020

Finding a Face

Finding a Face

a wounded woman
a man named Job
and a loving God of the unexpected

KRISTI L. MILLER

ISBN: 978-0-578-23194-5
Library of Congress Number: 2020905114

Library of Congress Cataloging-in-Publication Data

Names: Miller, Kristi, author
Title: Finding a Face/ Kristi L. Miller
Copyright © 2020 by Kristi L. Miller
Description: His Publishing Group, Includes bibliographical references

HISPUBLISHING GROUP

Division of Human Improvement Specialists, llc.
www.hispubg.com | info@hispubg.com

To Tom

I dedicate this book to you my beloved
husband who demonstrates unfailing
love, who gives me wings, and who remains
the greatest human gift
that God could give to me in this world.

And to my precious family
who have loved me just as I am.

And to all who have shared in this
story.

Contents

Acknowledgments

When I began to write the story of my face, I did not anticipate how many people would contribute along the way. Some were active players in the plot. Others joined in as I wrote this story.

Thanks first go to those who provided writing tips when this book was in its infancy. Mary Henderson, Katie Ellis Beam, and Janet Roberts took my rough drafts and gave me tracks to run on, inspiration to tell my story visually, and practical corrections.

Finding Donna Richards was the gift for my book to actually become a book. I will not forget our conversation one late afternoon in her New England home as I explained the drama of my story and shared my passion. "I want the reality of who I am and my walk with God during a dark time not to be made into anything other than what it was." She got me, my not so pretty story, and that was crucial to keep this story true. Her writing skills transformed my raw thoughts and loosely written chapters at last into book form.

A tremendous "thank you" goes to LeAnne Hardy who tirelessly provided crucial editing chapter by chapter, to ensure that they made logical sense while she made countless corrections and recommendations. I appreciated her comments when something I was trying to say seemed awkward or confusing, and I laughed when I read her honest reactions to my experiences. Her recommendations as to what was salvageable and what needed to be left out was greatly needed.

Jennifer McNeil not only became my final editor, but her important suggestions of filling in gaps and providing a more thorough back story, especially about my family, added another dimension. My face story related to my entire deeper life story which I needed to remember. Her comments and deep questions helped me know when and where to explain more for the reader's understanding.

I also thank our four children—Jonathan, Stephen, Leaza, and Scott—for their encouragement and candor. "Mom, we need to hear your emotions, your heart, your soul." Thanks for your invaluable wise advice as you read through my many pages and provided insightful recommendations regarding the book's design and marketing.

༄

Above all, I thank my beloved husband Tom who walked with me through this journey which became not just mine alone but ours together. This book came into being because of his strong support. He sat with me for countless hours on many an evening and weekends as I wrestled with trying to express in words not only what happened but how I was really feeling. He encouraged me to press on and fought for what I was fighting for as I wrote about Job and his suffering—that people would see God in darkness and be encouraged to run to God with their very real and many times not so positive thoughts and feelings. I am grateful that Tom ensured that my internal voice remained central to the telling of this story.

Introduction

If you don't get anything out of this story except to seek and hold onto God in the midst of darkness, then I have succeeded.

I have no idea what your darkness is, has been, or will be. I don't know how long it has lasted, is lasting, or will last.

I hope I will convey to you two things: the magnificence of the concept of following after God in the midst of darkness as well as the terrifying fear that you or I might not find God in a tangible sense in the midst of the darkness. Fear not. He is there.

My facial loss was an unexpected trial. It took me on a crazy journey. Family, friends, medical staff, and a whole host of people became involved along the way. I changed names, descriptions, and locations (except for my family) to provide anonymity as I wanted the story to be central.

As I went through this dark time physically, emotionally, and spiritually, there were times when I felt like I was grasping for God and couldn't sense him. "Where are you, God?" I often asked.

There is a cliché that asks, "If you don't feel close to God, guess who moved?" The insinuation is that if you don't feel close to God, you are the one who has moved. You are to blame. You are at fault. The implied assumption adds that anyone trying to seek God will always sense him. We have been told there is a formula: if we read about God enough, pray to him enough, follow him enough, walk in the Spirit enough, go to a place of worship enough, try to show faith enough, then we will always sense him tangibly.

However, countless men and women of God have experienced silence from God. The saying does not take into consideration that God is just as alive when he shows up in a still, small voice or when mountains are quaking, as he is when he willfully chooses not to reveal himself at all.

This book is also for those who cannot find God.

People often describe a time of personal darkness as wandering in a thick fog, trudging through a wilderness experience, being stuck in the desert, or experiencing the dark night of the soul. They can vividly describe feeling lost, alone, isolated, misunderstood, helpless, depressed, fearful, terrorized, desperate, disequilibrated, broken, at wit's end, and without a sense of hope, resolution, or answers

This is the story of a portion of my life that was hard. During the darkness, I befriended the biblical person of Job. I thought he could help me, for his response to deep suffering and incredible loss was recorded with openness and candor. Job did become a really good friend. I hope he will become yours, too.

God works in mysterious ways.

As you read my story, I hope my one little walk with God will help bring you to find him again as you are. No vending machine do I offer. "Put in the right coins and out comes exactly what you want." No formula either. "If you do such and such then God will do such and such." God is unpredictable. He works behind the scenes. He works in chaos. He does the unexpected.

As you also know, life is messy. It's a cocktail of beauty and the repulsive. There are days so joyful we think we will never be sad or discouraged again. There are days so discouraging and traumatic we wonder whether we will be able to have normal life once again. And there is a lot of the in between.

God is not just in the midst of answered prayers, times of triumph and discovery, and watching our dreams come true. He is in the midst of broken hearts, unfulfilled yearnings, and tragic loss. God is in the midst of everything.

He knows every nuance of your life. As someone said, "God knows you to the deepest depth, and He loves you to the skies."

May this story remind you of God's love.

During our lifetime we write two books.
The first is the Book of dreams.

We write this book when we are young,
when our life stretches before us, and
we can't wait to get there.
It is packed with excitement, adventure, and romance:
it is filled with anticipation, a prophecy of
everything we want to be and do.

We write the second book as we catch up with our future.
This it the book of what we really
become and really accomplish.

This is the Book of Reality.

Ron Dunn, *When Heaven is Silent*

Chapter 1

ↄ

A Thursday

It was a dark and stormy night. No, that's not true. It was a sunny early morning in the spring. My stomach and fingers were tied in knots as I sat in the reception room at the doctor's office. Despite all the research I had done, all the articles I'd read, and all the Internet searches I investigated, I distrusted the wisdom of the choice I was about to make. I turned to my husband, grabbed his hand, and spoke, my voice shaking.

"Tom, I could die from this, you know. I don't want to go through with it. But I don't want to lose the deposit either."

The night before, I saw every hour on the clock. I took my restless self down to the family room and overdosed on infomercials—the kind that describe the miraculous benefits of various cosmetic creams and "magic potions." I had recently joked that the more expensive the facial lotions I tried, the more quickly I seemed to age. But the long night viewing caused me to wrestle with my decision. *Maybe try one more serum? That way perhaps I could avoid having my face lasered in the morning.*

The ride to the doctor's office at 7:00 a.m. on that beautiful, blue-skied spring day had not been fun. Adrenalized by fear, I earlier expounded to Tom every concern and my back-and-forth confusion.

"I think I should wait. What will people think of me? But I need to get this done and over with. Remember, my sister? She almost died when she was kept under too long during a cosmetic procedure. If I die today, what will people think of me having this surgery done? And worst of all, what will happen to you and the kids if I die from a stupid laser? It's not worth it. I'll just tell Dr. Anders I can't go through with it. But I need to do something!"

Tom tried to encourage me. "Honey, you've thought this through a ton. I think you've made a good decision. It'll be okay. I know you're feeling scared, but try to relax."

◠◞

I could predict the future. Long before aging was anything I thought much about, I knew what was in store for me. The women on my side of the family did not age well. We all carried some sort of ultra-aging gene that wreaked havoc with our skin when we crested "the hill," despite enjoying youthful appearances prior to middle age. I used to joke with close friends, "Well, the women in my family look a bit haggard when we get old, but we seem to live forever." *I will most likely be the haggard looking one someday,* I thought.

But I still wanted to look as good as I could for as long as I could. My grandma actually lived to be over one hundred.

The men in our family, of course, seemed to defy the aging process altogether, looking decades younger even in their advanced years; my father was a prime example. My dad's face was devoid of wrinkles well into his eighties. So unfair.

While growing up, little emphasis was placed on looks in our household. My mom was adamant that what mattered most about people was their character and not their outward appearance. She actively discouraged vanity and noticeably never commented on looks. I always felt like I was the plain one, the middle daughter of three girls. My older sister was known for her beauty, and my younger sis was adorable and always photographed well. It didn't surprise me that she became the homecoming queen in high school. Overly self-conscious about how super skinny I was, I tried to hide in the shadows, rarely speaking out in school. I didn't mind being invisible. Of the three girls, I inherited my mom's genetics the most. I wished I had inherited my dad's instead.

I actually felt pretty good about how I looked by the time I turned twenty. I had figured out what hair color (blonde), what hairstyle (longer than shorter), and what clothes (trendy and form enhancing) made the most of my natural features. Like most women, I wondered how I measured up compared to others.

As a junior high teacher in southern California, my youthful looks sometimes confused parents. One fall afternoon during a parent-teacher conference, one of the mothers came into my classroom. She asked me, "Excuse me, where is Miss Munson, the history teacher?" (Munson was my maiden name.)

"I am Miss Munson."

"No, I want to talk with the actual teacher. I have a parent conference with her."

"I am the teacher. This is my class."

"This isn't funny. You can't be a teacher. You look too young. Are you sure?"

"Yes, I'm quite sure. I am actually twenty-two years old. Your son is in my world history class."

Despite the indirect compliment, there was a slight sense of foreboding during my younger years, knowing I was going to inevitably look old for my age. Yet I decided I might as well savor my youthful looks in the moment and enjoy the present.

Two short years later, I left teaching in California and moved to Indianapolis to work full-time with high school students in youth ministry. There I met my love and future husband, Tom. We first talked in August, began dating in November, quickly fell in love, and became engaged on Valentine's Day. We were married later that year on a hot August afternoon. Together we enjoyed married life and had four wonderful children. I was often told during those fun and exhausting years as a mom, "You look way too young to have four kids." I would smile and say, "Thank you!" Those words were nice to hear.

Chapter 2

◠

The Incalculable Riches of Crazy Days—The back story to my story

I did love being a mom. Exhausted, yes. Crazy busy, yes. But worth every minute. Our first-born, Jonathan, seemed to cry twenty out of twenty-four hours a day. A rough start. Nothing was wrong with him. He was just a super fussy baby. It wasn't until our second-born, Stephen, was old enough to sit up and play on the floor with him that Jonathan calmed down. I always felt Jonathan just wanted to be grown up already, but was stuck in a baby's body.

Stephen, born twenty-one months after Jonathan, was so calm when I brought him home from the hospital that I thought something must be wrong with him. I could actually lay him down for a nap, and he would fall asleep without a peep. I soon realized he was a very easy going baby. As he got older, he and Jonathan played quite well together—perhaps too well at times.

⁂

One afternoon, after packing for a trip, I called Tom. "Guess what, I am totally ready to go on tomorrow's retreat. All the suitcases are lined up …" And just as I said those words, I turned around to discover that Steve was covered from head to toe in red. Apparently Jonathan had managed to get the cap off of a large tube of my red acrylic paint. Not only did he paint his brother with his fingers, but he also had painted the wooden coffee table, sofa, and carpet as well. "Tom, you need to come home. Right away. Can you rent a carpet cleaner on the way?" As I grabbed the boys and we headed to the bathroom, I told Jonathan, "Both of you will stay in here until I get this mess cleaned up." As I left, Jonathan looked quite concerned about upcoming discipline. No time for that now.

Acrylic paint, unlike oil paint, dries within 10 minutes. I feverishly first scrubbed the sofa and carpet. Once I got most of the paint off of the various surfaces, I cleaned up Steve and Jonathan. Tom soon arrived with a carpet cleaner. We spent a few hours that evening trying to remove the red paint. Unfortunately, the red hue would always remain in the carpet. Such is life with children. It is marked with indelible stains.

⁂

Our daughter Leaza came twenty-one months after Steve. We called her "endless joy." No, the boys did not dote on their sister. As typical siblings, they had skirmishes. Leaza loved playing by herself and trying to do whatever her brothers were up to. When baseball became a major part of our lives, Leaza would sit on the bench with Tom and me and occasionally hold out her hand to her dad. He would give her a quarter to get an Airhead candy from the concession stand. She eventually enjoyed keeping track of the baseball players on score sheets.

Scott, our last, was born two and a half years after Leaza. So at one point we had four children ages five and younger. I wanted it that way. Because I didn't like the fragile baby phase, clumping the kids fairly close together was a good fit for me. Still, having four children felt a bit overwhelming. I could juggle three balls fairly well. Four seemed unwieldy. However, life soon became manageable even with the four. Scott was a fun, energetic, and upbeat addition. He became a Lego-lover and very imaginative kid, much like his siblings.

We had lots of laughter and fun in our home. Even though we had clear boundaries with quick discipline, we also allowed for flexibility and our children were given a voice. Our bedtime routine was a highlight for all of us. In the dark, before we said our nightly prayers, Tom would sit on the floor by the boys' bunk beds as I sat with the two youngest, and Tom would make up stories full of adventure. "Once upon a time, there was a great white horse, eighteen hands high who lived in an exotic land ..."

I hated it when Jonathan went off to kindergarten. Every afternoon the three younger siblings and I waited at the front window for him to get off the yellow school bus. I wanted to "freeze frame" our family in time.

It didn't surprise me that during the year when Scott went off to kindergarten that I sank into a bit of depression. How I missed having the children around. Because I wasn't sleeping well at night, I would get Scott off to school early with the rest of the kids, and then go back and nap the morning away until I picked him up at noon. It helped when I found another mother struggling as I was. "Let's meet on Fridays and run our errands together." How refreshing it was for us to meet weekly to commiserate. She drove while we both talked about our families and our lives. Fridays became a highlight and helped me adjust to life without children around during the day.

⌒

Sports and activities for the boys (soccer, baseball, track, basketball, and band) and for Leaza (gymnastics, flags for band, and synchronized swimming) throughout the years kept our calendars looking like a war-room strategy map. Tom and I were not at every practice and every event. And at times we got mixed up in our schedules. "Mom, this is Steve. Basketball practice ended twenty minutes ago. Did you forget to pick me up?"

Tom and I, like all parents, were navigating uncharted territory every day. By the time the kids were in high school, Jonathan and Leaza switched their focus from sports and became very involved with the marching band. Leaza was in the band as a flautist, primarily so that she could hang out with her friends and swing the flags with beautiful agility to help with band performances. I think the only time we heard her play her flute was before the chair placement tryouts each semester.

Jonathan became a superb percussionist. Right before his senior year, his voice suddenly went out just as he was ordering a meal at Wendy's. He tried to speak his order but all he could do was whisper. After weeks of misdiagnosis, we finally found an ENT who sent a tiny camera down Jon's throat. Voilà. The doctor knew what was wrong. Jon's vocal cords were flaming red and only one was moving. "Your son's vocal cords have been attacked by a virus. There's nothing we can do but hope they will eventually recover on their own." So, for many weeks, Jonathan struggled as he could only whisper directions to the drum line. At last one day, he came home from school and announced, "My voice came back much better as I was driving home from band practice today." Wonderful! That night our family joyfully thanked God that Jon could speak normally once again.

Late one afternoon we got a phone call that Steve had possibly received a concussion when he was undercut during a practice game for basketball. Steve loved basketball and played as the starting point guard his senior year. After returning home from the hospital, Steve spoke of feeling a bit rattled during practices. Tom and I prayed for wisdom as to what might possibly help. Tom decided to take Steve out to our local park and have him run the hills to see if his head felt weird in a different outdoor setting. After a few short runs, he said that he felt fine and not dizzy at all. Thankfully, Steve began to feel fully comfortable on the court once again and finished out the season playing as aggressively as he always did, fearlessly driving to the hoop, and fouling out on occasion.

Scott also enjoyed playing basketball in high school, but when he knew he would get little playing time his senior year, he decided to quit. I had an idea. "Tom, since Scott likes to stay busy and could use a creative outlet, would you teach him guitar?" Sure enough, not only did Scott pick up the guitar quickly, he soon put his skills to good use by helping lead worship for local youth groups. We never knew what church Scott would go to each week, but we were glad that he was involved in activities where not only did he have a purpose, but where he also had youth leaders who could provide some wisdom.

We were far from a perfect family. One evening, all four of our teenaged children seemed to be at odds with Tom and me and with each other. Tom said, "All right, everyone up to our bedroom." Upstairs, he grabbed a wadded up sock. "Okay, only the person holding the sock can speak." The kids laughed. After each held the sock and had his or her say, Tom took the sock and gave a conclusion. "So, your mom and I haven't been perfect parents. We had to pay for our own counseling. You'll have to pay for yours someday, too." We all burst out laughing. So true.

Chapter 3

⚬

Avoiding the Inevitable

Our four children taught me some of the lessons I, naturally being an introvert and low-risk person, so deftly avoided growing up. However, despite not taking big risks in public, I was a high achiever in private. I'd do anything to get a top grade or earn a badge. I also was not a bad tennis player, having taken tennis lessons for a few years.

After playing tennis with my dad one evening, the country club tennis coach came up to us on the court. "I would like to have your daughter consider joining our team this coming Saturday." As Dad drove me home, I felt terrified. *Surely, the coach only wants me on his team so that he has one more player. I'll look so bad compared to the other girls. There is no way I'm trying out.* For the next few days Dad tried to encourage me as best he could to at least see what it would be like to work out with the team. Fearful thoughts once again flooded my mind with potential embarrassment. *I've never been on a team before. What if I make mistakes? I'll look foolish if I don't play well.* "No, Dad, I'm not going."

Looking back, I often felt sad remorse for hurting my dad. He often took risks, and was a star athlete in high school and college. He told me in love, "Kristi, I wish you didn't have so little confidence in yourself when it came to sports."

⟨⟩

So, as the boys began competing for their school teams, I had to embrace a high learning curve. After Jonathan missed a basket during his first official game in middle school, I told Tom, "We should stay up here in the stands until everyone leaves because our son made some mistakes. It's embarrassing to disappoint the school team."

Tom incredulously responded. "Kristi, how many NBA players miss baskets when they have five guys going after them?"

"Ohh. Yeah, you're right." I had a lot to learn.

I admired our children for taking risks and learning to succeed and fail whether in sports, music, or other endeavors. Competing in public where hundreds might watch was comfortable for all of them and great for me to see. I was learning that risk isn't bad, and quite necessary for success, and the results would rarely ever be perfect. Just like life.

I often felt stressed watching our children playing sports. But for me, gymnastics was the hardest one to watch of all. *Why did Leaza have to pick such a precarious sport?* Every little wobble, misstep, or wrong move becomes a deduction. Plus the extreme pressure at meets is over the top. My hands would shake as I held the video camera.

Vault, bars, beam, and floor—all were places for potential injury. Falling off the bars while trying a new routine, Leaza experienced a severe arm break with a dislocated elbow. She couldn't compete for six weeks. On another day she almost sustained a broken nose.

Leaza and I prayed daily as we drove to gymnastics that she wouldn't have a serious injury. After breaking her foot just as she began her last gymnastic season, she recovered quickly enough to qualify for State and Regionals, so she ended her final season well. What a relief when she switched to synchronized swimming. Tom sometimes joked, "At least Leaza can't hurt herself if she falls into water. Perhaps drown maybe …"

⁓

During the years of raising our children, while they were trying new things, I mixed in my need for teaching, learning, and creating as well. As a former schoolteacher, I soon realized that I enjoyed researching and writing biblically and practical life-based studies for women on a wide variety of topics. As we moved through the years, I found a variety of places to speak, to teach, and to write.

As a mom with little time for myself, Tom often encouraged me to take art courses and to get out of the house. So on some evenings I could be found in art classes—painting, using oils, watercolors, or pastels with other students. I eventually got an associate degree in computer aided graphic design. In the beginning of this endeavor I didn't even know how to move the cursor, but in the end I loved looking at a white computer screen, knowing that I would have fun tweaking a photo in Photoshop, or using an Adobe program to create a unique image.

I love that adventure of art. During a sculpture and paper making course, Scott had to sit for hours while I made a clay likeness of his head. The sculpture of Scott's head still sits on a shelf in his bedroom. My world opened up with new ways to be creative.

To mix things up I took a few writing courses from our local adult continuing education center. How fun to discover that a former Hollywood screen writer was teaching my screen writing course. I had a blast writing a romantic-based murder mystery.

One of my driving passions has been to help others with pre-emptive life learning. One summer, I taught a neighborhood study on how to love our children so that they feel valued. I also taught a few courses on healthy leadership development. One of my favorite adventures, was writing and teaching an eleven part series I called "Finding God in the Midst …" Together our women's group looked at God in the midst of our work, our money, our romance, as well as God being in the midst of our pain and suffering, our failure, and even in our darkness.

Today our home has stacks of paintings leaning in corners, creative projects placed in closets, rocks displayed in cabinets (Tom's hobby), and a few guitars (Tom's love of playing) sitting in various rooms. Books are double-stacked in bookcases reflecting both Tom's and my love of learning. Saved letters are stored in boxes. Family photos sit on top of our unused piano and decorate our walls. All contain glimpses and reflections of what matters to us—God, family, friends, beauty, wonder, learning, and creativity.

Chapter 4

✐

Foreign Lands:
Life Lessons

All families go through difficult times. I could name a multitude of mishaps, challenges, and losses, and as one my friends said, "My husband and I could write books on what we did wrong in raising our kids." Our family took one major adventure when Tom was given the opportunity to help open up a high school ministry in Budapest, Hungary. Our time there would forever impact all of our lives.

Scott was three, Leaza was in kindergarten, Steve was in first grade, and Jonathan was in third. After going through eleven weeks of overseas training in California, we arrived in Budapest on a cold, snowy day in January. Our plan was to stay for a short stint—one to two years. Once we settled in, I tried homeschooling for two weeks. Being a former teacher, I felt it would be a practical way to get started until we got our footing. However, without any other children nearby, we soon realized this was not going to be a good option for our kids. They loved being with other children. Thankfully, our language tutor discovered that there were two girls in Steve's and Jonathan's grades who were fully bilingual, so we decided that our kids would go to Hungarian schools while Tom and I took Hungarian language classes in the mornings.

To sum up our time during the first year, Tom flourished working with high school students who went to schools that were English based while I dove into learning the language. However, Jonathan and Leaza both became visibly depressed. Their depression didn't go away. For an entire year I felt horrible for their misery. Our family actually celebrated Wednesdays. "Yeah! We're half way through the week." Tom and I prayed a lot that the children would adjust. We felt like we had thrown them into the deep end of a pool without swimming lessons. I felt their deep distress.

The following year we ended up putting both Jonathan and Leaza into a private English- based school, and they soon became their normal selves once again. Meanwhile, Steve loved being in his Hungarian class and wanted to stay. When I picked Scott up from his Hungarian preschool at noon, he was always smiling. We assumed he was also enjoying being at his preschool. It wasn't until years later that he spoke of his personal misery. "Oh, no Mom, it wasn't fun being there at all. The kids made fun of me everyday on the playground for being an American."

⌒

When Tom was offered to take on a new role in Budapest and stay long term, he was really excited. Now I became depressed. There's a monumental difference between being overseas when one knows it will be short term versus staying a long time. I loved Tom. I loved our family. I enjoyed the wonderful team of people and the close friends we had made there. But I felt isolated. Being a communicator, I felt like my wings were cut off. We had originally committed to work in Budapest for one to two years, so now Tom and I argued every night after the kids went to bed about what we should do. It wasn't pretty. I insisted that Tom needed to consider other options. As much as I tried to embrace staying much longer, I longed to get back to the States.

After a few months of this miserable mess of indecision, one June day I received a phone call from our overseas prep-trainer in California. Matt needed help with a mission team coming in. "Yes, I can pick the people up and get them their needed supplies. We have a big VW van." I quickly added, "Matt, what do you think about when a husband wants to stay for a long term and the wife doesn't?" Matt's response was immediate.

"Oh, we would never send a couple overseas if they did not have the same time commitment. That's our view. We have seen marriages become really frayed when both partners are not on the same page. Would you like to come and work for us in California? We'd love to have you as part of our team here."

"Thanks, Matt. That's a kind offer, but what about people saying I need to stay since Tom wants to and is flourishing? What about trusting his leadership and submission?"

"I don't think this is a marriage submission issue. It's more of finding out of what is a win-win for both of you.

Each of you were called by God to do good works. If only one of you is using your gifts and the other isn't, then someone is not able to express their God-given workmanship. Ideally, I think it's best to look for a place where both of you can flourish and do good works that you each like to do."

When Tom got home and I explained my conversation with Matt, he quickly called him back so he could talk about what we should do in the future. After the call Tom concluded, "I guess we will head back to the States once our short term commitment is over. But I still don't know what I want to do." Meanwhile God "showed up." I had begun sleeping with a picture of our family on my chest each night. In the dark I begged God, "Lord, we need help." Sometimes on restless nights I would get up and look out through the bars of the windows of our home and pray to God, "Show us what to do in our confusion. Please Lord, show us the way to move forward. We feel stuck."

Later that week, Tom was asked to shuttle mail to the students working on a college English learning project from the States. So off our family went to Lake Balaton. It just so happened that evening, after eating Hungarian hotdogs near the lake, we met a professor from Dallas Theological Seminary whose son was working on the project. As we talked together he asked, "How long are you staying here in Hungary?" Tom responded honestly.

"We don't know. But as of this week, we know we need to leave. I'm not clear what direction to take."

The professor talked with us some more and then stopped mid sentence. "Let me think." Then he made a profound suggestion.

"I have an idea. I'm inviting both of you to come to a LEAD (Leadership Evaluation and Development) session. It's where we as a team at our seminary do intensive evaluations of people who are in ministry but are in a quandary such as yours. Here's my business card. We are hosting LEAD in Dallas in November. Please do consider coming." *Wow. What an opportunity for Tom and me to get some much needed direction.*

It just so happened that as we were leaving our house that morning, I grabbed an audio cassette by Chuck Swindoll, the pastor from our host church in California. As I drove home in the dark, Tom and the kids all fell asleep, so I dropped in the cassette. Pastor Swindoll began the sermon with profound words for me to hear. "The theme for today's sermon comes from lessons I have learned from working with my wife, Cynthia, as she has expressed discernment over the years." He spoke candidly about their marital disharmony at times when he wanted to go in a certain direction and his wife did not feel good about it. He admitted that his wife could see and sense at times what he could not. Many times her concerns were later confirmed. His talk made me wonder. *So, perhaps my concerns about Tom and me staying long term might not be so ungrounded.*

And to top off these remarkable set of events, later that same week a young Hungarian couple came over to our home specifically to ask Tom to train them for next year. "We want to take over when you and Kristi leave someday."

Interesting. We now had replacements for the work Tom was doing. I began to wonder. *Are these unexpected experiences possibly a triple confirmation from God as Tom and I are wanting to move forward?*

⟋⟍

In November, we did fly out to part of the LEAD in Dallas, and it was profound. We were both challenged by the staff in different areas of our ministry, family, and marriage. Most importantly, bottom line—Tom was given tracks to run on. As we were evaluated, the leadership made several suggestions. "Tom, we think that now would be a great time for you to be further undergirded for the next phase of ministry. We encourage you to pursue a master's degree." Flying back to Budapest from Dallas we both felt excited that we had been given some clear direction.

We finished out the year as Tom worked alongside the Hungarian staff. Good-byes would be hard. We had grown to care deeply for our friends in Hungary. After looking at several grad schools, Tom chose to go to DTS and that's how our family got to Dallas, Texas. What a change.

⟋⟍

Our children loved living in the suburbs with lots of other children to play and go to school with. We were proud of them "jumping" into American activities, although it took awhile for each of us to figure out life here in the Dallas metroplex. One evening I asked Tom, "Do you feel as weird as I do? I know we only lived in Budapest two and a half years, but I feel like I'm trying to figure out life as a new-comer to the U.S." Being fully immersed in grad school, Tom could commiserate but on a whole different level. "Yes, Kris, I do. But each week it's getting better, isn't it?" Yes, that was true.

⌒⌒

Our marriage paradigm radically changed as a direct result of our difficult time in Budapest. Tom and I were both committed to become more of a team in our marriage, especially when it came to making hard decisions. While compromises are important at times, together we tried to look for options that would be a win-win for both of us. And we tried to listen to each other's hearts.

We were learning that healthy teamwork develops over time, especially as we sought answers and solutions to important issues regarding our work, our family, and our personal concerns. Tom and I had no idea how absolutely crucial our teamwork would become when my face and my life encountered an unexpected time of trauma.

Chapter 5

⁊

Investigation

I usually didn't think much about my face on a daily basis. I was the five-minute makeup type. Put it on as fast as possible and get out the door. However, having lived in Texas and California where I enjoyed being outside, playing tennis, and going to the beach, my skin revealed increasingly more sun damage.

Indeed, the aging rogue gene was beginning to kick in. The skin on my face rebelled, finding new ways to wrinkle and sag all the time. I was never made to feel unattractive by Tom or anyone else, but looking in the mirror I felt betrayed by my face. Finally, as our children were heading off to college, when creams and serums failed to get rid of anything but my money, I started to give consideration to "taking measures."

Having grown up in California and now residing in the Dallas metroplex, I was familiar with the emphasis on external beauty. Within these cultural contexts, Botox and dermal filler injections, acid peels, and other specialized treatments may become a part of a woman's cosmetic routine and landscape, trying to forestall the inevitable. There are more aggressive offerings as well. I came to realize that many of the women I so admired for their youthful looks were not always that way naturally.

My mom had two face-lifts to ward off her sagging and wrinkled skin. This was less due to vanity than an effort to ensure employability as an adjunct education professor, which meant financial security in a world where youth is celebrated and where age is disparaged. My older sister had tried several different cosmetic procedures, often exhorting me to try them too.

Maybe I should think about it . . . No, I don't think so. Some of her experiences in the facial enhancing world included some scary complications.

I complained to Tom, "Look at all these wrinkles lining up on my face. I've never smoked, and I have smoker lines, too! You know Tracy? Well, she is five years older than I am, and she looks ten years younger. I think I need to do something."

Occasionally, magazines came to our home that advertised a variety of body and facial aesthetic corrective procedures. As I looked at photos of women's facial transformations, I liked what I saw. *Perhaps I'll try just one.*

But I feared doing any major facial treatment.

When Tom and I got some tax money back one spring, the scales finally tipped. I embarked on an investigation in earnest, seeking out real options to make a significant difference for my face. Being frugal, I wanted to find some procedure that I had to do only once. I could not afford a facelift. Many less invasive facial procedures required repeats, and those would not be an option for us financially. I needed to keep it low in cost. Keep it simple.

⟡

I figured a good place to begin would be with my personal dermatologist. The day I went in for a consultation, she sent me down the hall to talk with her top aesthetician. The young woman briefly looked at my face and said, "I can't really do anything here at this office to correct your problems. Your skin is too far gone."

"Really?"

"Yes, your skin is just so sun-damaged."

I felt discouraged. *Phooey . . . My face is as bad as I thought.*

She then made a recommendation. "Contact Dr. Karen Joy. She's a dermatologist who uses a special laser. Here's her number." As she handed me a business card, she encouraged me, "Her clients with skin damage similar to yours end up looking fabulous. They have beautiful skin afterwards."

A good start. I did some homework.

Indeed the procedure that Dr. Joy used, a heavy-duty skin resurfacing laser, offered a dramatic result, and it lasted longer than some other procedures. More bang for your buck. It would be ten years before retreatment would be required versus two to three years after less invasive lasers. Better results, longer lasting, less costly, and more convenient overall. It sounded good to me.

After extensive research, I found several doctors in the Dallas-Fort Worth metroplex who used the recommended laser procedure. Some had advertisements and websites that dazzled with credentials, and their colorful before-and-after photos were alluring. First, I called Dr. Joy's office and set up an appointment. The earliest she could see me was in a couple weeks. I also made appointments with two other doctors. The one who could see me first was Dr. Larry Anders, so on the day of my appointment the following week, I was off on my adventure.

Dr. Anders's website was impressive, and his office did not disappoint. The walls were adorned with bright Caribbean art along with a cascading water feature. The overall decor gave the place an upscale and relaxing feel. The receptionist greeted me with a warm smile and escorted me into a lovely inner office with large windows.

When Dr. Anders came in, he was dressed in a white lab coat. He was very energetic. As we discussed the issues I wanted corrected, he seemed knowledgeable and experienced. He handed me a massive book full of over a hundred before-and-after photos of his clients. As I flipped through the pages, I could see women with features and skin much like mine whose after-treatment faces looked much younger, fresh, and natural. *Wow, these women look great.*

This natural look was very important to me. First, I had very fair, delicate skin, which also had considerable sun damage, warranting careful treatment. Second, I did not want to look like some of those celebrities who end up resembling cartoon versions of their former selves. I just wanted a fresher, younger-looking me.

Dr. Anders made his recommendations. "Yes, I think you'll benefit from a heavy-duty laser. However, unlike other lasers you will need to have general anesthesia for this one. This one is much more invasive."

"Don't I need to go to a hospital for that?"

"No, we can do it here in the office."

"Are you sure?"

"Yes, I do it all the time, and I can do a small surgical procedure to tighten up the skin under your chin. The initial recovery will take about ten days, and all the redness will fade after several weeks."

Several weeks? I thought about it. *I want to look good for Scott's high school graduation in early May. This is March 7th. I need to get moving on this, and fast.*

I now considered not seeing the other doctors with whom I had set up appointments. After all, this doctor seemed to know what he was doing and promised me just what I wanted.

The pictures speak louder than words. Yes, I think I will do the laser procedure with Dr. Anders.

This quick decision was highly uncharacteristic of me. Usually I thoroughly checked out all options before making an important decision, especially one of this magnitude. But time seemed to be of the essence, and I was overcome by a wave of hopefulness, trusting in Dr. Anders and his great pictures. So with excited anticipation, I "seized the day."

Anders walked me out to the front desk. As we checked the schedule with the receptionist for the first available opening, she happily responded, "We actually have an opening tomorrow morning. You'll need to put down a non-refundable deposit today."

I needed to make a decision. *Why not get this over with tomorrow? The sooner the better.* "Okay, let's do it." I wrote out a check and handed it to the receptionist.

While Dr. Anders and I both considered the open appointment good fortune, the receptionist suddenly questioned him. "If Kristi comes in tomorrow morning, she will not have taken the required prophylactic antibiotic twenty-four to forty-eight hours prior to the procedure."

He spoke assertively. "That won't be a problem."

The receptionist gave me instructions. "Okay, Kristi, be here by 7:30 tomorrow morning. Here's your prescription. Wear a top that you can zip or button from the front so it will be easy to put on after the procedure is done." I came home and cancelled my other two consultations. Full speed ahead for a fresher, younger-looking me.

Chapter 6

ↄ◯

D-Day

Sometimes our darkest hours begin in the light of day. Now it was D-day. As I nervously sat with Tom in the reception area, Dr. Anders' face on the front of his glossy promotional magazine smiled back at me, reassuring me that I would no longer look old for my age. I would soon have a younger-looking complexion. Yet, I continued to recount to Tom the fears that swam through my head. "I'm so scared. I'd like to walk out of here and just go home. But, I've already given the doctor my deposit."

Tom reassured me once again. "Kristi, I'm supportive of whatever decision you make. Let's just talk to the doctor when he gets here. I am sure he can answer your questions."

I was grateful to have Tom by my side as my friend and confidant. We had been married for twenty-seven years, and I knew he loved me just as I was, wrinkles and saggy skin included. Like most men, I knew he appreciated that I tried to look nice, but both of us knew that what truly mattered about a person was the inner self.

Soon Dr. Anders calmly walked in, wearing his scrubs. I anxiously explained some of my fears and trepidation about moving ahead. He reassured me all would be well, but it would be my decision.

"Okay. I'll go ahead with it."

His young medical assistant escorted me to the dressing area. I changed into a blue hospital gown and entered the brightly lit operating room. They set up my IV.

Fade to black.

∽

I awoke groggy and dazed. My first thoughts were joyful ones. *I am alive! I didn't die! The worst is over!*

As I sat on a medical lounge chair, Anders handed me a mirror. Staring back at me was a very strange person. My entire face was covered with white mesh except for slits for my eyes, nose, and mouth. I looked like a mummy ready for Halloween. Under the mesh lay a facial dressing called second skin. I was glad the doctor would remove it the next day and show me how to cut and apply the bandages myself. When it was time to leave, I was helped into a wheelchair. A staff member pushed me while Tom and Dr. Anders walked behind.

The doctor spoke proudly of his work. "I was very aggressive, taking three layers of skin, even four in some places. I expect a very dramatic result."

The medical assistant wheeled me down to the main lobby. While Tom went to retrieve the car, I sat in the huge waiting area feeling a bit odd. *What do the people passing by think of me with my ghost-like appearance? Surely no one could possibly tell who I was.*

I imagined I looked like one of the famous Hollywood movie stars, all bandaged up after having major facial work done. I was hopeful that the result would be just as I anticipated.

⟡

That night in bed I shivered uncontrollably as the anesthesia wore off. I sat propped up against the headboard because I was not supposed to lie flat for the next few days. Tom stirred fitfully beside me, feeling my jitters and sensing my unease.

While my body processed the after effects of the anesthesia, and I felt the onset of pain, my mind resumed the gymnastics of the night before, jumping all over the place with worries and regrets. *What have I done? What was I thinking?* I even thought, *What if I look too young?*

I felt miserable and vulnerable, and the more my face hurt, the more I questioned having done such an invasive procedure. As I sat there in the dark, quivering and scared, I couldn't cry. And I couldn't scream. My face hurt too much, and I didn't want to disturb my sleeping husband further, so I climbed slowly and shakily out of bed. As I swung my legs over the edge, I talked to God in the darkness.

"God, I really need you."

I had been a believer in God since I was a little girl. Growing up, I was taught that Jesus loved me so much that he died for me. After I trusted Jesus to become my Savior, God always seemed to be a present and an integral part of my life—through good times and bad. I talked to him all the time about most everything. I told him exactly how I felt. "God, I'm very scared."

I was no stranger to sharing my pain with God. I knew that anyone who lives long enough will experience deep pain and loss. Tom and I had experienced the pain of a miscarriage, dealt with financial distress, had wrung our hands watching a child deal with depression, and wrestled with many a quandary, especially as our children traversed their teenage years. Often we did not know what to do. Yet in the midst of these hardships and trials, I always had a sense that God was with me—watching, caring, and present.

As I climbed out of bed, I had the odd sensation of God's presence leaving me like a big, strong black bird flying off into the night. At this moment I suddenly felt completely alone. This unfamiliar and disturbing, almost inexplicable feeling would become part of the journey I was now beginning.

Shivering in the dark, I made my way to Leaza's bedroom (she was away at college), and spent the rest of the night sitting up in her pink upholstered rocking chair. I propped my feet on the side of her bed and looked out the window to the night sky. I dozed on and off. Morning would come and so I hoped, would relief.

Chapter 7

Go-To Is a No-Go

Tom and I worked for a non-profit faith-based organization focused on bringing humanitarian aid and the message of God's love to others in need. It had taken us to people around the world. Two days after my procedure, Tom flew out to lead a ten-day trip to Belarus where much of the fallout from Chernobyl's nuclear accident decades ago had ruined their lands. His group was bringing aid to the local people while visiting schools, hospitals, and homes for the elderly. Leaza was excited to join the team during her spring break.

I was looking forward to hearing stories upon their return about how the humanitarian aid and spiritual hope had made a difference in people's lives. I assumed that by the time they returned to the States my face would be pretty much healed. In the meantime, my two companions were Scott, our high-school-aged son, and our Scottish Terrier, Winston.

While Tom was away, I enlisted the help of friends to drive me to Dr. Anders' office for my aftercare. "Pick me up in the back alleyway," I suggested. It was a characteristic of Texas properties to have alleys in the back of homes instead of garages in the front. I had never quite understood why, but now I was grateful for them. With the alley in back I could avoid my neighbors witnessing my comings and goings, and perhaps wondering, "Who is that masked woman?"

⟡

Each day at Dr. Anders' office was an exercise in endurance. He would remove my bandages and use a 20/80 vinegar to water solution to clean my face. Ouch! Then he reapplied the second skin material and covered the pieces with gauze until the following day. After a few days, I noticed that the bandages didn't stay in place. Each morning the pieces slid down my face under the gauze and almost fell out onto my neck. Weird.

Dr. Anders seemed puzzled as he looked at my face. "This has never happened before. Something must be wrong with the bandages."

"*Never happened before.*" Just what I wanted to hear.

On Sunday when I changed my own bandages, I saw a white colored film across my entire forehead. I was concerned, and so on my Monday appointment I told Dr. Anders exactly what I saw. "Is this normal?"

Simultaneously, he began to question me. "Have you had problems with your skin healing before? Does your skin heal slowly?"

"No," I replied. "I can't think of any time when I did not heal normally." Then he rebandaged me for another day.

I became increasingly concerned with his continued bandaging and questions.

Having thoroughly researched the heavy-duty laser procedure, I knew that the postoperative instruction recommended that bandaging be used for no more than two to four days. I had read articles noting that "repeated bandaging beyond the recommended time period could lead to infection and result in scarring." Some experts suggested no bandaging at all.

So on the fourth day, I gave a printed copy of one of the articles I had collected during my facial research to Anders, as I questioned his bandaging protocol. "What do you think?" He gave the paper a cursory glance and put it into his file.

As he looked at my skin, he said, "Your skin is not reepithelializing as it should." I had no idea what that meant, but I assumed it was not good.

He bandaged my face two more days for a total of six. Finally, on Wednesday morning he threw up his hands and reluctantly sent me home without the second skin bandages. His final comment was, "Your skin is healing too slowly."

⟨⟩

By that afternoon, things were not looking good. Yellowish fluid was coming out from the pores in my face. It slowly ran down from my forehead and collected around my eyebrows. I consoled myself. *I don't need to worry. My skin is probably just overreacting as it's exposed to the air. Let's see how it does tomorrow.*

I spent that night propped up on the love seat in our family room in the same spot where I had pondered the procedure during a similar restless night. The fluid continued to ooze down and around my face and started to get near my eyes by morning.

On Thursday morning, I washed my face and applied the recommended moisturizer. Again, I tried to be positive. *The fluid will stop this time.* However, by afternoon the yellow goo was still coming out of the pores of my forehead, my cheeks, everywhere. *This is getting ridiculous. I'd better call the office and see if I can come in right away.*

⁓

Calling Dr. Ander's office proved aggravating to say the least. He was supposed to be my resource as my physician. Unfortunately, my go-to was a no-go. I began with the receptionist.

"Hi. This is Kristi Miller. Umm . . . after I got home yesterday, my face started oozing a lot of fluid and I'm quite concerned. Could I come in and see the doctor?"

"We're closing the office right now."

"Well, could I come in tomorrow?"

A cool reply. "No. We will not be in the office tomorrow."

"What about someone else? Could I see one of the medical assistants?"

With irritation, the receptionist responded, "I've already told you. No one will be here tomorrow, and everyone in our office is going on vacation for the next five days. Come in for your scheduled appointment on Tuesday. Here, I'll let you talk to the doctor."

I now tried to explain my concerns to Anders directly.

"Dr. Anders, I know you told me to put moisturizer on. The problem is my face is leaking so much fluid, I don't know where to put it."

"Just wash and moisturize your face once a day, and I'll see you on Tuesday as scheduled."

He apparently handed the phone back to the receptionist.

She curtly closed out our conversation. "'See you Tuesday, just as I told you before."

I hung up the phone.

Really? That's it? Is this really happening? No response or course of action? No doctor to call in his absence? No medical staff to help me?

My heart sank. Tuesday seemed so far way. It was Thursday. What was I supposed to do for the next five days? I felt utterly abandoned, like I was stranded on an island alone with a storm coming, and the last boat had left. Not only was something very wrong with my face, but now I was left all on my own to deal with it.

Chapter 8

✑

Five Fearful Days
and a Smelly Face

Something was wrong—very wrong. I just knew it as I sat home alone. The next five days seemed interminably long. Between the combination of terror and physical pain, I was kept on high alert, although I felt totally exhausted at the same time. I called a good friend, Mary, who happened to be home recovering from a much less invasive laser procedure. She was going nuts with itching. I was going nuts with the fear of the unknown. We commiserated.

Thankfully, Steve came home from college over the weekend. As I talked with him regarding my predicament, he blurted out, "Mom, your face smells." Not exactly what I wanted to hear.

I voiced my despair. "I know. I think I have a bad infection, but I'm afraid if I went to a hospital they wouldn't know what to do. My raw face would frighten everyone who saw me, and Dr. Anders said I needed to wait until Tuesday."

I counted down the days one by one. All weekend long I restlessly tried to sleep either propped up against the wooden headboard upstairs or against the back of the love seat downstairs.

As my face drained this strange fluid, my pain level swung between uncomfortable and unbearable. I resolved to try to negotiate a Monday appointment. The office staff were supposed to return by then, and I didn't want to wait until Tuesday if I didn't have to. I had a plan.

⌒

At last Monday morning came. After checking my face in the mirror to confirm that it was still having issues, I called the office. I was surprised that Dr. Anders' receptionist was open to me coming in a day early. "We have an opening at two this afternoon. You can come in then." *Finally some help.*

I called one of my closest friends, Jane, whom I hadn't seen over the past few months, and asked her to give me a ride. We had known each other for thirteen years (since our family first moved to Texas) and had taught English as a second language together. It was always easy to share our highest highs and darkest lows with each other.

Just as Jane pulled into our driveway, I walked out the back gate. I could see her concerned face through the windshield. At that moment, I burst into tears. I couldn't stop myself. I instantly leaned my head downward so my tears fell onto the hot cement rather than down my cheeks.

Something about seeing my longtime friend opened the floodgates.

"I know I look scary," I wailed. "Thank you so much for coming to help me." Jane showed no negative reaction to the strangeness of my appearance. She just kindly helped me get into the back seat of her car. As she drove, I explained the saga of the past few days. And I wondered what Dr. Anders would think when he saw my face.

⌒

Arriving at my two o'clock appointment, I approached the receptionist's desk. Dr. Anders happened to be standing nearby. His eyes widened as soon as he saw me, and without a word he whisked me out of the waiting room and into an inner office. He sat me down on a medical chaise lounge, and still without talking, began washing my face with the vinegar solution.

He seemed to huff and puff as he lightly rubbed and scrubbed my raw skin. The excruciating pain made me doubt the wisdom of his actions. After several minutes, he finally spoke. "I was able to wash away about a third of it."

What does that mean? I wondered. *Whatever is wrong with my face, which is probably an infection, it can't be washed away.*

"I want you to come in twice tomorrow, once in the morning and once in the afternoon. I'll soak your face with a 50/50 vinegar to water solution for two twenty-minute sessions."

Whoa. The thought of going through another rubbing and scrubbing treatment with an even stronger concentration did not sound pleasant. *But what else could I do? I have to go back.*

Jane volunteered to take me to the torture chamber the next day. As soon as I arrived, the doctor swabbed a sample of my "yellow stuff" to send it off to an infectious disease lab. He said that he had consulted with another doctor who recommended that a culture be taken.

About time.

The next day, I once again lay down on one of the lounge tables. Dr. Anders wrapped my face with cloths soaked with the strong vinegar solution.

Yikes, my face is on fire! I can feel every pore throbbing with every beat of my heart! This is crazy!

Lying there for twenty minutes, I really began to dread having to come back again in the afternoon to do this all over again. Alternating between wanting to sob and wanting to scream, I lay quietly still. Neither option was available to me.

What a great relief when Anders came in and removed the cloths. I could now recover from the pain. Then he reminded me, "You will need to come back again at 2:30 for your second treatment." My relief instantly faded.

After lunch I faced the inevitable once again. This time, when Anders placed the vinegar-soaked cloths on my face, it seemed like my body wanted to go into shock as the pain increased exponentially. Every pore felt like it was on fire, piercing and throbbing. In my misery, I tried to think. *This is a stupid idea. This can't be doing much of anything. Vinegar won't get rid of an infection in the skin. How much more can I endure?* As the solution soaked in, my face felt like it was swelling, stretching to the breaking point. I couldn't bear much more. My only comfort was Jane sitting nearby.

Dr. Anders at last returned to remove the cloths. "I am prescribing an oral antibiotic. Just keep taking it." He seemed unclear as to what to do next. He handed me the prescription and said nothing more.

As Jane led me out of the office and to the elevator, I held up a reddish colored hand towel with two holes I had cut out of it in order to see where I was going. I thought that the hand towel would be less scary for the people in the medical building who might happen to see my face. As we waited for the elevator, I could feel the weight of the day pressing in, making me tired and despondent. *Oh my goodness. This is horrible.*

Jane guided me into the elevator as I almost walked into the adjacent wall. A nicely dressed young woman came in with us. I felt embarrassed that she had to see my creepy-looking face. As we all left the elevator, she said to me, "Honey, I don't know what happened to you, but I am praying for you."

I was touched by such kindness. "Thanks so much." *I really, really do need your prayers.*

As Jane and I walked arm and arm to the parking garage, I felt like a puddle of a person. I wanted to fall down in a heap, feeling worn out, stressed out, and pained out.

⌒

Back at home, I tried to avoid looking at my face all evening, fearing what I would see. My skin felt like an overly inflated balloon, ready to burst. Yet around midnight I forced myself to look in the bathroom mirror. I winced. Looking back at me was someone who looked as if she had been used as a punching bag. My face was swollen, red, and damaged. And I could feel the yellow fluid coming out more than ever.

I sat propped up all night, once again asking God for help.

"God, I am so alone. I wish Tom was here. He's so far away and I don't even know where he is in Belarus. Even if I could contact him he couldn't help me anyway. Please show me what to do. I'm in big trouble."

One thing I did know—Dr. Anders wasn't the answer. I needed a new direction . . . a different doctor. As I didn't sleep all night, I mulled over my options. I resolved to call Dr. Joy, the dermatologist who had come so highly recommended when I was first checking out laser procedures. I prayed repeatedly to God in desperation, "Please, please, please God, please let her be able to see me when I call in the morning."

Morning took forever to come.

Chapter 9

"Can Someone Help Me?"

After a mostly sleepless night, I waited until 6:30 a.m. to call Dr. Joy's number, knowing I would get her answering service. I quickly spilled out the nature of my emergency and dire need of help. The woman on the line responded, "I'll contact Dr. Joy and relay your issues."

Hanging up the phone, I became instantly fearful that my new plan was probably a dead end. I seriously doubted whether Dr. Joy would take me on as a new case, especially on such short notice. *At least I was in her system,* I consoled myself. I waited. I prayed fervently, "Lord, please do the impossible. Let Dr. Joy be willing to see me."

Within minutes, the receptionist called back. "Dr. Joy said that she is willing to see you this morning, but you must be at her downtown office by eight." It was 6:45 a.m.

⟨𝒪⟩

My elation quickly turned to panic. *Oh my goodness. Now what? I am not allowed to drive. Who can take me this early in the morning?*

I decided to call Julie, a longtime friend and neighbor. I thought she might be up because she liked to walk her dogs early in the morning. She was awake! As I explained my urgent need for a driver she immediately offered to help. I hurried over to her house through the back alley on my early morning mission.

By the time we left, we hit rush hour traffic big time. I began to panic inside as we moved sluggishly along the freeway. *We're not going to make it to the office by eight.*

Tom happened to call my cell as we sat amid the sea of cars. This was the fist time I had been able to talk with him since he left for Belarus. "Hi, hon, we just got back to Chicago. We had a great time in Belarus. How are you?"

I gushed, "Not so good. Something is wrong with my face, and I am trying to see another doctor, a Dr. Joy. Julie is driving. We're stuck in traffic and I'm supposed to be there by eight."

Tom said, "Let me pray." He prayed for me and for the traffic to open up. Not long after, it did just that. I only hoped that we would still make it in time.

We arrived in the parking lot of the medical complex at 8:12 a.m. I bolted out of the car, looking like a crazy woman, not knowing exactly where Dr. Joy's office was located. As Julie parked the car, I ran into the office lobby and to my great relief, I quickly found her name on the wall roster. I rushed to the elevator. After exiting, I ran down the hallway. But by the time I arrived at the office it was already 8:15. Not good. The receptionist was the only one there. I apologized profusely for being late, explaining the circumstances, to which she responded, "I think you are too late, but I will check."

As I sat all alone in the waiting room, I prayed again. The receptionist returned and stated without emotion, "Dr. Joy said she will see you." I felt so relieved that I almost burst into tears.

ᴄᴏ

Just then Julie arrived, and together we were escorted to a brightly lit inner office with a window at the end. When Dr. Joy came in, she took one look at my damaged face and declared, "You have a staph infection." I felt instant relief to know that she knew exactly what was wrong. *Finally, someone had confirmed what was going on!*

A lovely dermatologist both in appearance and demeanor, Dr. Joy took some time to discuss what was happening and what would happen next. Her experience and encouragement were both reassuring and comforting. She said that in all her years of practice, she had treated only one other patient who had a small area of staph. "That woman healed fully without any scarring." *Dare I hope that I would not only find a remedy, but I might not be scarred?* Elation!

Dr. Joy looked at my antibiotic prescription, changed the potency, and then added some other medications. She explained the protocol and what to expect. "Once you are on the right antibiotics, your skin will form a hard crusting shell which will blacken and then fall off in about ten days." She instructed me to wash only the exposed areas once a day, cautioning, "I know you will feel tempted, but do not disturb the crusting on your face. Never remove it or you will be scarred." She further warned, "Under the crusting is staph. Do not touch it as your skin will slough it all off. It must be left alone."

I couldn't have felt more relieved when Dr. Joy offered to contact Dr. Anders personally. "I will explain to him the protocol that needs to be done. But Kristi, I want you to continue to see him periodically, as he will finish your case." I didn't like that idea, but I resigned myself to it.

"Thanks, Dr. Joy, for being willing to see me on such short notice."

"When I got the call this morning," she replied, "I was thinking, 'What if this woman was my mother?' I would want someone to help her."

I left the office with a lightness in my heart. Dr. Joy had been so gracious to me. I was filled with hope this all would soon be behind me. *Ten days from now this frightening situation will all be over.*

Chapter 10

✺

Helmet Face

Back home, Tom called saying that his flight had arrived in Dallas and that he and Leaza would be coming home shortly. "How was your appointment?"

"I found out from Dr. Joy that I have a staph infection. She has upped my antibiotics and given me some other meds. She said the fluid will form a hardened crust. I want you to know that I look really scary. Please tell Leaza so she won't be too shocked."

I braced myself. When Tom and Leaza arrived, he came into the house first. As he walked into the entryway, I came out from the family room to greet him. Tom stopped dead in his tracks as soon as he saw me and just stared at me with a look that can only be described as shock. Leaza peeked around his side. They didn't move for a bit and then cautiously walked toward me to see my face close up. They both hugged me from the side and told me how much they loved me. Their touch was most welcome as were my Tom's sympathetic words: "Oh, baby, I'm so sorry."

By the next day, just as Dr. Joy predicted, my face fluid stopped and formed a hardened crust. I literally could not move my face at all. It felt like an attached encasement, like a medieval knight's helmet had been glued onto my face. "The woman in the iron mask." I could blink my eyes and open my mouth, but just barely.

Our neighbor Julie dropped by to see how I was and offered to feed all of us dinner. As we enjoyed the meal, I tried to eat, but nothing seemed to fit into my mouth. Luckily, she made some string beans and they fit perfectly. That was about all I could eat that night. *I'm going to have to get creative now that I have to live with a frozen face for the next ten days.*

✂

I quickly realized that in order to eat, I now would have to ingest almost everything through a straw. Yogurt, applesauce, liquid vitamins, and protein drinks would work. Only a certain size straw got the job done easily. The fat straws used for milkshakes were the best.

Tom suggested that we get tacos from a local restaurant called Taco Delight. Indeed they were perfect—ground beef, minced lettuce, minced tomato, and the thin crispy taco shells—the ingredients slid easily between my lips. Tom had always been a huge fan of the local eatery with all their fresh ingredients. Now I became a fan as well.

For variety, Leaza soon introduced me to Jamba Juice. She ordered me a delicious blueberry-based drink with extra protein. Jamba Juices of various flavors became an additional bonus meal. These treats helped to keep my spirits up.

✦

One evening, as our family gathered to watch a fun comedy, I quickly realized that normal laughing was now out of the question. Whenever a hilarious scene came on, I quickly left the family room to avoid laughing at all because moving my face was so excruciating. But I learned I could laugh by saying, "Ho, ho, ho" with rounded lips, sounding kind of like Santa.

Later that week, my younger sister called and told me a sad story, and I winced with my forehead. *Ouch.* Now expressing empathetic emotions also needed to be avoided. I was grateful that my face hurt only if I moved it too much.

Crying was pretty much out of the question, now too. Too complicated. Crying involves moving many parts of the face, and I knew it also wasn't wise to get any tears on the crusting. When I felt like I wanted to cry, I learned to lean forward and let a few tears fall into the inner corners of my eyes where I would quickly dab them with a tissue.

Brushing my teeth became a new adventure. I could barely fit the toothbrush into my mouth. I had to be ever so careful as my face could no longer stretch.

I soon discovered that sneezing was the absolute worst. When I sensed a sneeze coming on, I grabbed both sides of my head to keep it from moving as much as possible. Still, with each sneeze my entire face jolted with pain.

You know how you get goose bumps when you watch someone win a difficult race, hear a tender story, or listen to some beautiful music? Well, when I felt those kinds of emotions, I now could now actually feel every pore in my face. It was pretty cool feeling goosebumps where I had never felt them before. So, there was one interesting benefit of having an encrusted face.

⌒⚬

On Friday I received a call from Dr. Anders' office. "The lab report has come back. You have a staph infection called *staphylococcus aureus*. The antibiotic you are taking should work." I quickly googled staph aureus ("golden staph" due to its color). So that's why when the fluid would come out of my skin, it looked yellow. Thankfully this staph strain wasn't as dangerous as the strain called MRSA (which is resistant to antibiotics and can be life-threatening). Nevertheless, staph aureus could be very virulent. I was grateful to know there were several antibiotics that could be used in the arsenal to fight it.

⌒⚬

I knew that I needed to let my family know right away about what had happened, but felt weird telling them, "Hey, I got a bad staph infection when I had my face lasered and now my face is a wreck." When I finally called Mom and my two sisters and told them that I had complications from a laser procedure, I could tell from their responses that none of them fully understood the extent of my facial damage. Hearing that someone has a staph infection might seem as if they have a rash, so I sent them close-up photos of my face so they could see firsthand what I was dealing with.

My older sister, Kari, fully commiserated. She had experienced a major facial setback years ago. In her case, when a doctor removed the loose skin from her eyelids, he took off too much skin from one lid. So, her right eyelid did not have enough skin to fully close. She spent months looking like she had one normal looking eye and one "fish-eye." The follow-up treatments were complicated, eventually requiring a second surgery. She had to apply an ointment to her eye for about a year. So, Kari intuitively understood the gamut of my emotions, especially my fears now that my face was in danger and I didn't know what would happen next.

My dear mom, who lived in Seattle, was dealing with significant health problems of her own. She had recently been diagnosed with advanced and aggressive breast cancer, but her outlook was amazingly positive and upbeat. At the time, she was visiting her brother and sister-in- law, getting some much needed R&R near the beach. I asked my aunt to show Mom the photos of my face that I had sent in the mail. She warned Mom as she handed her the pictures, "You're going to be shocked."

Mom immediately called. "I'm so sorry, Kristi. Please let me know the latest developments. I am very concerned." Later that week she talked about my condition with my dad so he would know. Due to his Parkinson's, my dad lived in a group home near Seattle. After Mom returned home, she and Dad began to pray for me in earnest.

When my younger sister Lauri, who also lived in the Seattle area, showed the pictures of my face to her husband, he responded, "Who is that?"

"Kristi."

"No, it can't be."

I was unrecognizable. I felt like I had been thrown into a lost world that no one could understand.

Chapter 11

⁓

I Matter

Letting other friends know about my plight was not easy either. It might seem strange, but one afternoon I asked Leaza to take a picture of Tom and me in the backyard with my new monster-look so I could use it as a visual to show others. Because Tom and I work for a Christian nonprofit, each month we send newsletters to our ministry friends and family. I told Tom, "I feel kind of embarrassed asking for prayers about getting a staph infection from doing a beauty-related procedure. I hope they don't think I'm vain. But we do need to let them know about this serious situation so they can pray." Tom fully agreed.

As we took the picture in our backyard, I tried to smile. Impossible. So Tom and I added a funny bubble caption with the picture, saying, "But I am smiling," and included it with our newsletter.

⌐⌐

I had a major epiphany during this time. I had always assumed that if I were to die, apart from my family, I would leave a mere trace in this world. I envisioned a very small funeral service with only family members and a handful of others in attendance.

It's not that I didn't know my life was valuable just as a human being. Of course it was. I also knew that I had taught children, teens, and adults throughout my life with passion, prayer, and care. Whenever I began writing, designing, doing a piece of art, creating, I usually would begin my projects with, "Lord, help me with this." I needed God's wisdom and creativity through all aspects of my life. Above all, I felt my greatest joy and accomplishment was being a wife and a mom. Most recently it had been encouraging to watch our young adult children take off and learn to live life on their own. But now looking back, my life seemed like a short blip on the screen. Had I really made much of a difference?

I was about to be shocked.

Within a few days of sending out our newsletter, Tom and I received an outpouring of kindness and support from friends and family. Phone calls, letters, cards, e-mails, and gift cards came to us from all over the country. We received compassionate messages of encouragement and offers of many, many prayers.

As I read each letter, e-mail, and card (some accompanied by flowers), I held them to my heart. I thanked God for each person who cared about me. I no longer could tell myself that I didn't matter. I read words like, "I can't believe something like this would happen to someone as special as you." *Wow.* Gestures of kindness from good and caring people gave me comfort to carry on, to fight, and hopefully get to the other side of this predicament. *I am not alone in my suffering. Many people are pulling for me, praying for me, helping me get through.*

So my chosen lie for decades, the lie of my insignificance, died. I now told myself a new truth. *Kristi, you've been so foolish. Your life does matter, not just to God, but to so many others. What a destructive lie you have listened to all these years. This was not how God ever wanted you to think about yourself.*

One late afternoon, my friend Betty called me. With raw emotions she spoke, "I just had to call you. I drove up to my mailbox today, grabbed the mail, and for some reason I decided to open up your newsletter right away. As soon as I saw the picture of your face, I burst into tears. I couldn't drive for a while. I just sat in the car crying." I was incredibly touched by her words. Betty understood how scary the journey was that I was on, and her call meant the world to me as I struggled.

Tom was getting much-needed encouragement as well. Several men who had received our newsletter contacted Tom directly, expressing their deep concern for both of us. They knew he was on the difficult, uphill battle with me, and he needed their support.

One afternoon, I received a large package in the mail. Inside was a colorful blanket from a girlfriend in California. Christina's note explained, "This blanket comes with our love and prayers. We are praying that your skin will heal, and that your face will have no scarring." It was signed by Christina and several women. I felt deeply humbled to receive such a beautiful gift.

One of my former college roommates sent me a beautiful card. I laughed out loud when I pulled out the enclosed gift card for Victoria's Secret. I felt far from "womanly" at that moment, but my dear friend Tammy was sending me a message of future hope.

⟳

During this unexpected outpouring of support, I reflected on the needless grief that comes from lies we believe. We believe so many different lies. I was reminded during this time of individuals who feel like their lives have little value due to a major setback or crushing experience. If only each could see how many people would want to express love and deep concern, and provide a vibrant testament of their worth, declaring, "Your life matters."

I thought back to one of my dear friends who spoke of her father's suicide. He was the owner of a failing company and did not have the heart to lay off his thirty employees. So in great anguish, he took his own life. His daughter said, "Wouldn't you know it, within a fairly short time each of those people had found another job. Dad took his life so needlessly. He left a hole in our family that could never be filled." His life really did matter, whether he had a failing business or not.

I also thought about a beautiful woman I met at a copy store years ago. As she arranged pictures of a handsome young man on a large poster board, I became curious. "Are you making a display for your son's graduation from high school?"

"No," she responded. "These are pictures of my son who committed suicide in college two years ago. I am part of a grief group for those whose loved ones have died due to suicide, and I am doing this project in honor of him. He committed suicide because his girlfriend broke up with him." I felt heartsick for this dear mom.

"I'm so very sorry to hear that," was all I could say.

Later, I thought about the tragedy. Yes, how terribly sad. I so wished that her son could have discovered that his life mattered even when the love of his life had rejected him. If only he had given himself the time to see a future where he could experience love again, where he could see his incredible value, and find life and hope again. Now his entire family lived with a profound sense of sadness and unrecoverable loss. This young man's life mattered.

Then I thought of our friend Greg, whose wife had left him after a two-year affair. He was devastated. The past couple years had been grueling for this father of three. But recently he had begun dating and was beginning to enjoy life once again. He told Tom and me, "All I could see then was what was in front of me. That's all I knew. But now, life is opening up once again."

There is an abysmal and gripping darkness that often comes with a major loss, debilitating pain, personal failure, rejection, or the loss of a role of personal significance. The lie is that this black hole is all there will ever be. Greg had been able to set aside the lie in his life. Now I had set aside some of my lies too.

Leaza gave me a wooden tray for Mother's Day. "I think it will come in handy as you spend time sitting on the sofa." That tray became the perfect place for all the letters, cards, and the emails that Tom brought home from the office. And the overflowing tray became a beautiful testament for me to see each day. Even on the darkest of days it would remind me, "Kristi, you are loved. And you matter."

Chapter 12

⁣ↄ

What Are Friends For?

As I walked through the pain and fear of the unknown on a daily basis, local friends became an invaluable blessing. Some dropped off meals. Others dropped by to show their support. I didn't mind when some of our closest friends who came to visit stood far away from me, as if I had the plague. I assumed they felt shock and legitimate concern about catching whatever I had. Staph was a dangerous and kind of a creepy infection, after all. But their willingness to visit despite their nervousness showed they really cared. Their presence lifted Tom and me. We didn't feel so alone.

One lovely Saturday afternoon, my friend Natalie came over to run some errands for me. As we sat in the sunny family room and chatted, she handed me a dark pink journal. "Perhaps you can use this."

"Thanks! What a great gift! I'll be able to write down what I'm learning while on this journey." Off she went to get the items that I had written down on a list. The pink journal would become a quiet friend, and and a precious place to process my thoughts and emotions.

⌀

Later that week Tom came home with an opportunity. "Ruth (the human resource director) wants you to try to join us at the spring staff retreat."

"I can't go, Tom. I look so ugly. I'll scare everyone."

"I think it would be a good break for you. The staff really love you, and I know they won't care how you look."

Because I wasn't able to get out much except for doctor appointments, I consented. I even began to look forward to being with people I knew and being out in nature.

Setting out from home late one afternoon, I lay in the backseat while Tom drove. I held a towel over my head the whole way so the sun's rays would not hit my crusty face. When we arrived, Ruth and several of the staff met us at the car and walked with us to the evening meeting to hear the speaker. Tom and I took seats in the back row of the large meeting room. I couldn't believe how refreshing it was just to be out with friends. Several staff members came over to greet us, while others who sat near us didn't talk with us at all. That didn't bother me. I figured they were being polite and giving me space.

The next day, some of Tom's coworkers came by his office to ask, "Who was that woman who sat with you at the retreat? Was she a friend?" When Tom explained that it was me, Kristi, they were astonished. "We are so sorry!

We didn't recognize Kristi at all! Please apologize to her for us." Their apology wasn't needed. I completely understood.

❦

As I stayed on the latest round of antibiotics, I became increasingly aware that my body was not happy. Yet these meds were my only hope for a full recovery. I tried to explain the odd feeling to Tom, Dr. Anders, and to Dr. Joy. "When I take my antibiotics, it feels like my heart wants to stop beating. I feel as if my body will just quit." Neither of my doctors had any answers. I don't think they could figure out what I was trying to convey.

All I knew was that on Saturday afternoon, while using the computer upstairs while Tom had gone to his office, my body seemed to want to shut down once again. *There it goes. I feel so . . . so, so what? I don't know. I've got to get downstairs to the folder with Dr. Anders number on it! Something's wrong again. He said that I could call him if I had anymore issues with my meds. I've got to call him!*

Grabbing my cell phone and hanging onto the railing, I crawled down the stairs, and managed to get to the kitchen. I took the folder off the counter and collapsed onto the kitchen tiles. I called Anders' receptionist in utter panic. Soon, he called back. After hearing my desperate concerns, he said, "You can go off of one of the antibiotics, but you must stay on the other." As I sat on the floor crying, fearing I might die, I called Tom at work. He rushed home, and thirty minutes later found me sitting on the kitchen floor.

He said, "I think we should head to the hospital." We decided since I hadn't eaten well for days, that we should first stop at a Wendy's. Sitting in the parking lot, I slid whatever was thin—a slice of bacon, tomato, lettuce, and some fries—between my teeth to try to get my energy up. As we discussed our options, I said, "I think I'm feeling better now. Let's see if I have another issue again. Let's go home."

I told Tom that evening, "I am not staying home any longer when you go to the office. I feel too fragile. I don't want to keep calling you to come home."

My thoughts reflected back a few years when a dear friend had suddenly passed away from taking a mixture of prescription and over-the-counter meds when she was only a young mom. I added, "If I am going to die from reacting to my meds, I want to die looking at the back of your head."

⁓

Tom got permission for me to come with him to the office. So, on Monday morning I brought a cushion, a small blanket and pillow, and created a little spot behind Tom's door. It was a smallish space, and because Tom disliked overhead lighting, his desk lamp kept the room feeling cozy and comfortable throughout the day. What a strange way to live. But I could fully relax there. In the comfort of his presence, I rested from the exhaustion that came from lack of sleep and the toll that the infection and medications were taking on my system. That corner behind his door became a safe haven for me in the midst of my storm.

Chapter 13

‿○

Warning! Warning! Warning!

Meanwhile, Dr. Joy encouraged me to continue seeing Dr. Anders to show him my progress. I dreaded the visits to his office, but I did as she suggested.

When he saw me, Anders would ask various questions. "Do you have a dog who has an infection?"

"No"

"Do you work in a garden?"

"No."

"Have there been times in the past when your wounds healed slowly?"

"No."

I think Dr. Anders was trying to figure out why I had not already healed. He clearly felt strongly that something was wrong with me or with my living environment. I could tell he was searching for answers, but I thought he was missing the most crucial point. I now had staph deep in my skin, and it needed to heal from the inside out, just as Dr. Joy had indicated.

On one of the visits, he and one of his assistants approached me. "I think we need to do something with your face."

I made it crystal clear. "You can only look at my face and not touch it until the crusting comes off. That's what Dr. Joy has said."

Anders then asked me, "Can I have permission to take pictures of your face?"

"Sure, that's okay." As he took photos, I thought about how "funny" it would be for some of them to appear in one of his large books that had all the before-and-after pictures. Somehow I didn't think he'd want to advertise my particular "dramatic results."

The ten-day process of "crust blackening" meant that I had two doctors to see on various days. I asked friends to come up the back alley to pick me up and always forewarned them. "I look awful. Don't be too scared." They never showed any shock upon seeing me. They drove me to the offices and engaged in conversation as if I was a normal person. I appreciated that my friends willingly helped me even while knowing of my serious condition of having staph. I don't know if I would have done the same.

As each of the ten days went by, I anticipated better days. *This will soon be over. I will be so glad not to bother*

*people any more and no longer have to worry about this
disaster on my face.*

Sure enough, one evening while reading in the family room, a big chunk of the loosened crust fell into my lap. Normally I would be grossed out by such an event, but instead I was thrilled. *This is working! And it's day ten, just like Dr. Joy had said.* Looking into the mirror I saw that my skin looked normal underneath. *Wonderful! Thank you, God!*

I visited Dr. Joy the following day. She was very pleased. "I am so proud of you, Kristi, and how careful you have been to leave large portions of the crust hanging on without disturbing them. They kind of look like large dark shells moving as you speak. I don't think I would have had the patience you have shown to leave them all alone." She added, "You may now wash the exposed skin with a mild cleanser." With her blessing, each evening I gently patted one area of new skin with a paper towel and threw it into the trash, and then did the same for each of the other areas to avoid cross-contamination.

Much more of the crusting began to fall off in various sized portions, freeing my face more and more from its encasement. I was very encouraged and eager to fully heal and be done with this mess. Little did I know that I was about to take a huge step backward.

⁓

I had faithfully visited both doctors for the past two weeks. Whenever Dr. Anders and his medical assistant looked at my face, I continued to make it clear, "I'm not allowed to have the crusting disturbed." By Friday afternoon, after much of the encasement had fallen off, I drove to Ander's office, thinking that he would be very encouraged to see how well my face was healing. The crust was now reduced to a few small places along my left jawline, still covered about 40 percent of my forehead, and remained stuck on both temples.

As I sat back in the lounge chair in the treatment room, Anders offered to wash my face. I thought it would be fine, as I knew Dr. Joy had explained to him what should and shouldn't be done.

But before I knew it, he and his assistant took out some soaked cloths and began rubbing my entire face. As they swished the cleansing cloths around more vigorously, I instantly felt both shock and terror. Frozen by disbelief and despair, I finally found my voice.

"You're hurting me."

I was ignored. They kept on rubbing my face. I could feel the scabbing being pulled away. And, as a grand finale to his abomination of treatment, Anders finished by swiping my entire face in a circular motion with an ointment.

"There, I have put a topical antibiotic on your whole face. That should do it."

Stunned by what had just happened, I couldn't believe what this doctor could possibly have done. *What if he's just messed up my face—again?* My shock, fear, and immense vulnerability turned to fury. I had told him on several previous occasions that my skin was not to be disturbed according to Dr. Joy. He had not listened. I mumbled something about needing to use the bathroom. When I looked in the bathroom mirror, I felt sheltered. There was no crusting left on my face at all.

Everything had been going as it should, and the past ten days had not been easy. Could Dr. Anders have undone it all just like that?

∼

When I got out to the car to look at my face close up in the rearview mirror, sure enough I saw little specks of fluid coming out of countless holes on my forehead and along the jawline where the scabs had all been removed. My temples were bleeding, which explained why it had hurt so much. My lower right jaw had a small area that was bleeding too.

My mind screamed. *I should have never gone back to see you, Dr. Anders! What were you thinking? What was I thinking to trust you?*

When I got home, I tried as best as I could to stay calm. But once again I sat up all night again, dreading what my face might look like the next day. Still, I hoped that my fears would turn out to be unfounded. Another miserable night, waiting for morning to come.

Chapter 14

It's Baaack...

My worst nightmare looked back at me in the mirror on Saturday morning. Yellow fluid was seeping out of the reopened areas throughout my face. It was very difficult not to just lose it altogether. But because it was the weekend I had to sit tight until I could see Dr. Joy—hopefully on Monday. Not easy at all.

I felt so emotionally distraught that I asked Tom and Steve if I could ride with them when they ran a quick errand together. I didn't want to be home alone. As they both went inside an office building, I waited alone in the car in the empty parking lot. In the car's rearview mirror I could still see yellow fluid glistening from all the areas where the crusting had been prematurely removed.

At this point, "not losing it" was no longer an option. My utter distress simply came out. I screamed at the top of my voice, "God, 'I'm so messed up! I'm so messed up! I'm so messed up!" I wailed and cried out again, "Lord, I can't go through this again! Please. I cannot go through this again!"

I regained my composure by the time Tom and Steve returned. When Tom looked in through the back window, his face showed it all—empathy, frustration, and deep concern for me.

Unable to wait until Monday, I called Dr. Joy to tell her what had happened. She sounded dismayed and said, "I'll certainly see you on Monday."

Many fears floated through my mind and haunted me all weekend. *Would the infection ever end? Would I be scarred? What could be done now?*

I had been so very careful to follow Dr. Joy's instructions to a T. Yet, Dr. Anders in less than twenty minutes, had wiped out all that had been painfully accomplished.

Monday came. Tom and I both felt compelled to confront Dr. Anders before we saw Dr. Joy later that day. I wanted him to see firsthand how the infection was coming out of the areas where he had removed the crusting on Friday. He needed to understand how his reckless treatment, especially after all I had been through, had thrown me back to square one.

Tom and I did not set up an appointment with his office. We determined to arrive early enough to speak with him before his first patients might arrive.

Tom dropped me off around 7:30. As he parked the car, I took the back stairway to avoid seeing anyone. I had my trusty towel with the two eyeholes draped in front of my face. I trudged wearily up each step. Peeking around the exit door, I could see no one in the hallway. I walked up to Dr. Anders' office door.

As angry as I was, I didn't have the emotional strength to go into his office alone, so I sat outside the door, crumpled on the floor of the hallway, leaning against the wall. I felt utter despair. *This is awful. I don't want to see this man again. But I have to.*

Tom arrived, helped me up, and escorted me in. After talking with the receptionist, we were told that Dr. Anders was willing to see me.

What transpired was a very unsatisfying and absolutely mind-boggling experience. I poured my heart out to Dr. Anders as he closely peered at my face.

"Look, my face now has staph coming out of all the places that you disturbed. I am so scared of what will happen next. I was on the road to full recovery and now I have to start all over again. I am very upset!"

Dr. Anders' grabbed my medical file and turned his back to us. When he turned back around, he declared, "I have made no mistakes."

I looked at him dumbfounded.

I told him, "I don't want you touching my face again."

He became defensive. "Apparently, you don't trust me."

That was an understatement.

"Why did you violate the protocol of a dermatologist who had successfully treated staph before?" I asked. "You said that I was the only case that you had ever seen, so why did you not follow Dr. Joy's instructions? She knew what would work."

Upon hearing our raised voices, the receptionist came into the room. Dr. Anders replied, "Another patient got the same infection a few days after you did," and then he added with emphasis, "And she is already healed."

I couldn't believe what I was hearing. He was actually admitting that another person got the same infection. How incriminating.

His angry reaction reminded me of the scene in the movie, *A Few Good Men*. It stars Tom Cruise as an inexperienced US Navy lawyer grilling the intrepid and legendary Colonel Nathan R. Jessup (played by Jack Nicholson). Finally, feeling utterly frustrated through the cross examinations, the Colonel screams out in the court room, "You can't handle the truth!" thereby divulging his culpability for the tragic death of a young marine.

Shocked by Dr. Anders' revelation and more shocked that he would admit it, I asked him, "Did this woman have the same exact laser procedure that I did?"

"Yes, she did." It seemed interesting that two of us got the same staph infection from the same procedure at the same office.

"Dr. Anders, I have never had trouble healing." I added, "It might have helped had you seen me when I first told you I thought I had a problem and not make me wait for five extra days."

Tom supported me, telling Anders how upset and frustrated he was as well.

At this point Tom and I realized that further interaction would simply be aggravating and go nowhere. We said our goodbyes, left the office and headed out into the unknown.

(Dr. Anders did call me once to see how I was doing. That was thoughtful of him. But I never saw him again.)

Chapter 15

Three Times Is Not a Charm

L ater that afternoon, as Dr. Joy studied my newly damaged face, she was very empathetic. She had already
called Dr. Anders to express how she felt about what he had
done. Sadly, she did not seem as optimistic as before.

I was now on a third round of antibiotics. The hope was
that the meds would once again clear the infection by drying
up the fluid and forming another hardened, black crust on
my face which would eventually fall off, leaving healed skin
in its place. But just as we feared, this did not happen.

And the antibiotics started to affect my health in
frightening ways.

One morning I ventured out to visit a dear friend, Erica, at her home. As we enjoyed a lovely lunch, I took my afternoon pill. Within five minutes, I began to feel sick. It's hard to explain, but I felt woozy not from being nauseous, but like my whole body was reacting to the meds, making me feel indescribably weird and very uneasy inside.

"I feel awful."

Erica became concerned as I felt increasingly worse, so we quickly got into her car and headed to the closest hospital. I thought I'd feel better as she drove me along, but instead I felt worse, like my body was shutting down. Erica kept saying to me, "Keep awake. Kristi, stay with me." I tried to stay cognizant.

When we finally arrived at the hospital, she walked with me to the admitting area to ensure I wouldn't collapse. I quickly explained my strange facial appearance and described my physical reactions to the meds to the admittance staff. They thought I was having a panic attack. I thought it was something far different. My heart wasn't racing. I felt just the opposite, like it was stopping. I wasn't feeling hot or sweaty either.

I was escorted to a hospital bed where they took my vitals. After the doctor questioned me he left the room. About thirty minutes after we arrived, they took my blood pressure again. It read 78 over 46. Extremely low. As I rested, I began to feel better. The medical staff offered no suggestions. I waited about twenty minutes more. They took my vitals once again and sent me home.

While Erica drove me back, I began to speculate. *I wonder if my body feels like it was stopping at times because the antibiotics cause my blood pressure to plummet. That makes sense. And perhaps my extremely low blood pressure makes me feel like my heart wants to quit beating. That makes sense too. But what can I do?*

$\mathcal{O}$

Job: The Beginning of a Long-Term Friendship

During my daily visits to Tom's office, I decided that I wanted to begin studying the book of Job. It seemed a logical choice. Job had endured suffering, and far more than I would ever experience.

Various people thought that it would be depressing for me to study Job's life, but I sought a comrade in suffering. I knew he had remained faithful to God despite his horrific losses, cruel mistreatment, and extreme pain. That's what I needed—this man's courageous example to give me perspective.

So I began with my study. Every day I went to the large conference room to read the book of Job. Concerned about knocking the crusting off in my temple area, I could no longer use my reading glasses. Instead I used a plastic magnifier and began writing down my thoughts in my pink journal. After a few days I found an old pair of glasses with a broken arm. Even better. I could now easily read without touching my damaged face.

I quickly realized that I wasn't blameless like Job was. Nor as passionate. After he lost everything, including his livestock, servants, and his seven sons and three daughters, he grieved and worshiped God with profound words. "The LORD gives and he takes away. Blessed be his name." I don't think I would have ever thought Job's thoughts if I had such horrific events happen in my life all at once. Basically, he was saying, "God, you are in charge. Everything I have been blessed with has been given by you, and even when you can take it all away, I will still bless you as my God." This was his immediate and natural response. Amazing.

I also appreciated that Job openly and passionately expressed a wide gamut of emotions and thoughts to his friends and to God. Many of his thoughts and feelings were neither pretty nor positive. I could relate. Much of the time Job begged God to step in and make it clear to his friends that his trials were not due to his personal sin. I saw the value of his candor. I had a lot to learn from this man.

Knowing I was in the midst of a difficult journey, I wanted to keep my life and my heart pure and open with God. I spent a number of days looking inward.

"Lord God, please show me if there are any strongholds of sin in my life that I haven't dealt with. Show me if there is any unresolved brokenness in relationships that I might need to resolve. Show me anything hidden in my heart that needs to come to light. Amen."

I wrote down various sins that I could think of. I also asked Tom whether there were sinful areas of my life that I needed to become aware of and also confess. Nothing hidden or monumental jumped out at Tom or me. I would continue to confess sins as they came to mind.

⌁

The best part of being at the office during this time was being with the staff who made me laugh and kept me distracted from focusing on the horror of my face. Many a late afternoon as I rested in the back of Tom's office, I took great comfort hearing the sounds of voices and the friendly banter in the hallways and cubicles not far away. What a calming place to be during my time of storm.

One morning, Tom asked me to join his team as they were having a planning meeting. "I think you could contribute some ideas." Having had a miserable night of little sleep and low energy, I set up my pillow and blanket under the conference table where Tom and some of the staff met. I listened to their discussion from below the table. Occasionally I would interject, "Good point," or "I agree," or, "I have an idea." We all chuckled. It's not every day people hear comments coming from down under a table. After while, I decided it would be best to sit in a chair to directly engage with the team, as we discussed the various issues. It was gracious of the staff to include me and they lifted my spirit.

The only bad part of being in Tom's office building was the giant mirror in the women's restroom. I dreaded going in there. The mirror literally covered the entire wall in front of both sinks. So it was impossible to avoid looking at my face. I didn't want to see myself if I could possibly help it. Seeing my reflection was a discouraging reminder of what others had to look at.

As I came out of the restroom one day, I ran into Bev.

"You know, maybe I could make some money off of my face. I could be in a horror movie and the makeup artist wouldn't even need to do my makeup." Bev laughed at me. At least I was trying to add a little humor to this disaster.

⟋⟍

During Easter weekend Leaza came home from college, and together we all watched a movie on TV. As we sat in the family room, I took my antibiotic and sure enough, ten minutes later I was gasping for breath. Leaza immediately asked me to show her the pharmaceutical pamphlet that came with the prescription. I gave it to her.

"Look Mom, it says right here that an indication of a negative reaction to this antibiotic is 'difficulty in breathing.'"

"I know. I can tell," I responded, "but we're trying to fight the staph infection."

Just as I fell asleep later that night, I was jolted awake, gasping for air every time I tried to lay flat. So I spent the night like a yo-yo. I ended up sitting upright in bed next to Tom, trying desperately to breathe. *Leaza is right. I have to go off the meds, and soon.*

The next day I quit taking the antibiotic that compromised my breathing, and I informed Dr. Joy. She was not happy with my decision, but I felt I was in a critical situation and needed to breathe naturally.

For the next two days I didn't feel that my breathing was doing much better, so Tom took me to the local urgent care clinic. Sure enough, the doctor discovered that my blood oxygen level was on the low end of what was normal. It took two more days for my breathing to finally return to normal.

I was now off all antibiotics, but my face was still a mess. I was still in danger.

⌒

It seemed whenever Tom was gone, unpredictable things happened to me and my face. On the following weekend, while he was on a trip in Colorado, I could see a marked difference in the intensity of the infection spreading up the sides of my face, even popping up in a few new spots on my neck, forearm, and lower leg. Because the staph resumed its party on my face and beyond without any antibiotics to stop it, I now had to deal with a whole new level of scary.

Thankfully, on Sunday evening our church home group was meeting together. I openly voiced my mounting fears. "My staph is getting worse because I had to go off my last antibiotic, and it seems to be threatening my eyes. I don't know what to do."

My friends gathered together and prayed for me with great concern and care. One of the men suggested an infectious disease doctor whom he knew at a hospital in the Dallas/Fort Worth area. He called me later that night with the contact information.

Needing new answers fast, I called the infectious disease office first thing Monday morning. I did not know if any doctor in the group would be able to help me, but I had to try. When I asked to see a doctor as soon as possible, the receptionist said, "The earliest appointment will be in three weeks. That's good, because normally it takes six weeks to get an initial appointment." Trying to remain calm, and knowing I was new to this office, I explained the severity of my situation. She put me on hold, and when she came back she said, "There is an opening on Friday." She seemed pleased.

That was certainly accommodating, but because of the rapid pace of the infection creeping quickly into new places, I pleaded with her once more "This is really serious. I am afraid the staph infection will have spread really close to my eyes by Friday." She put me on hold once more. I felt a little like a car buyer negotiating the purchase price for a new car, and the salesman keeps disappearing into the manager's office when asked for a better deal. I prayed hard while I waited on the silent phone line. When she came back, she said, "Dr. John Palik has offered to see you at two o'clock this afternoon."

I was elated and relieved. "Thanks so much! That's so helpful!"

My next phone call was to my friend Kelli, who graciously consented to take me to the appointment.

⌒

Dr. Palik's office was located downtown. When Kelli and I arrived, I once again used my face towel to get to the upstairs offices, trying not to scare those who might see me. As if holding up a hand towel with holes in it didn't freak people out.

Once in the waiting room, I noticed a wide variety of patients and their companions. The receptionist was warm and friendly, and she did not outwardly react to my scary face as I held the towel in my hand while signing in. "Just write your first name," she said. I signed in, assuming this infectious disease practice safeguarded people's identities, and sat down with Kelli.

When it was my turn, a medical aid escorted us into a small room with a large window. As I sat on the examining table, Kelli and I prayed together. "Lord, we ask that this doctor will know what to do."

Before long, in walked a tall, slender, pleasant looking man. Dr. Palik's demeanor was very calming. He listened attentively to my quick summation and reviewed my medical records, and then studied the list of recommended antibiotics. I explained my negative reactions to the most recent one which I had quit taking.

"I want to begin with the most mild antibiotics on the list," he said, adding, "We will start simple and work our way up to the more potent ones."

I pointed out the new places where it seemed that staph was showing up on my skin. "Do you see this spot on my neck and the one on my ankle?" He confirmed, "These are new areas most likely infected by staph, and I think it is becoming systemic." Not what I wanted to hear. He also cautioned, "Until all the scabbing comes off your entire face, staph will remain underneath. You need to be extremely careful not to have any breaks in your skin. Don't shave at all. And there is also a high susceptibility for toxic shock syndrome." He further warned, "Your skin should not be exposed to any sunlight, including reflections off the dashboard or even the cement sidewalks of Texas."

After I signed a consent form, I gingerly put the pen onto one of the tables in the room and said, "You probably won't want to touch that pen again. I feel like I am such a threat to others with this infection."

Dr. Palik explained that it was not all that rare for a person to have staph on their skin, and he didn't seem worried about me being highly contagious. That was a relief. Once my face was clear of infection, he would provide a protocol that would keep it away for good.

As we left the doctor said, "I wish my resident students could see your face. We just never see anything like this in America." I told him he was welcome to take pictures.

Now it was confirmed. I knew for certain what I had suspected all along. I was indeed an anomaly.

When I started the new antibiotic that afternoon I could almost sense it stopping the infection in its tracks. I spoke with Tom on the phone about the good doctor and the new direction I was taking. I actually went to bed smiling that night (as best I could at the time). Hope had not left me completely. *Perhaps my trials will soon be over.* "Lord, I thank you for this infectious disease doctor and that he actually seems to know what to do with my staph infection."

Chapter 17

∽

Monkey, Manuka, and Maggots

After his latest trip and knowing of my most recent set back, Tom brought home a gift just for me, a hairy, orange stuffed monkey. Tom always had a fun sense of humor.

"Kristi, this is my special gift for you. Whenever I am out of town, I want you to see this monkey and remember that I wish I could be with you. This monkey will be my representative when I am away, my pinch-hitter."

I fondly named the monkey, "Monkey." Monkey always made me smile. When Tom was home and took a nap, sometimes I placed the hairy creature on his chest and waited for him to wake up. When he woke and saw the goofy orange monkey staring back at him, he would laugh out loud. This fuzzy, crazy creature represented Tom's love for me and our close connection as a team.

To my great benefit, I was walking in this dark time with the full support of my life partner. Countless times Tom and I prayed together. Most of our prayers were basic. "God, we don't know what to do. Please show us what to do. And, dear Lord, please show the doctors what will work for Kristi to get her face back."

I have to say that there were no dramatic changes in my situation or even in my overall outlook as a result of our prayer times together. We pressed on after each closed door. Tom and I were coming together, going before the One who knew us, and who saw every nuance of the confusion and darkness we walked in. But more than that, knowing God cared about even the smallest of sparrows who fell, we knew he compassionately heard every one of our simple prayers. We would keep going to God as we took each step into what felt like a deep fog.

⟡

Over the past two months, Tom ended up transporting me and accompanying me to most of my doctors' appointments. He also had to pick up most of the chores at home and run all the errands because the doctors did not want me to do anything that would make me hot and cause my face to sweat. I was also not permitted to move around a lot where I might accidentally knock the crusting off.

I don't know how I would have handled the stress without Tom's tremendous emotional support. He became my extra ears at appointments, my cheering section, and my sounding board. Thankfully, he understood my fatigue, stress, fear, and despondence. We both were making major adaptations in our everyday lives and taking all precautions necessary for what used to be the simplest of activities— things such as eating, doing laundry, driving, and sleeping. Tom was leaning on God as best he could. I didn't hear him complain much, but he said he was complaining plenty to himself and to God. I was quite aware that this confusing and difficult time was happening to him too.

After work each day Tom had the car running and fairly cooled off by the time I hopped in to return home from the office. One lovely late afternoon, while riding in the backseat, ever mindful to protect my face from sunlight, my face seemed to be tightening more than usual. With a tear-filled voice I told him, "Tom, I feel like scar tissue is forming under the crust, making my face immovable. Something's wrong with it!"

While my head was still bowed in sorrow, I heard a distinct wail from the front seat. Tom was crying . . . crying for me, crying with me. My agony was his as well.

⟆

Sleeping together meant sleeping at times in opposite directions as I feared a wayward shoulder, arm, or hand might come in contact with my face. We could hold hands very easily as we slept in reverse to one another. Tom made it a practice to kiss me on the top of my head daily, tenderly, comfortingly.

One evening, as Tom was reading in one direction and I was resting in the opposite, I sat up to get out of bed.

Immediately I cried out! "I hit my forehead on your heel!" Apparently Tom had crossed one leg on top of the other. I rushed to the bathroom. Sure enough, the upper right corner of my crusting had been knocked sidewise. It looked jammed into my face. There was nothing I could do but cry. From then on that area kind of stuck out more than the rest of my forehead.

For the next few weeks, the mild antibiotic prescribed by Dr. Palik kept my infection stable. That was the good news. The bad news became evident when five weeks went by and the crusting just sat there. It seemed to be permanently imbedded in the deep layers of my skin.

✐

The event for which I had undergone this fateful laser procedure—our youngest son's high school graduation had arrived. Needless to say, the experience was different than I originally imagined. One might say it was surreal.

It now was mid-May and time for Scott's senior prom. One beautiful Saturday afternoon, he and his date were joining friends at a picturesque lakeside location to take pictures. I didn't want to feel left out of such an important occasion, so I had an idea. "Tom, I want to ride with you this afternoon when you go to take pictures of Scott and his prom group. Maybe I can somehow feel a part of all of this." Tom parked our van in a position where I could look out through the open side door and watch from a distance. As Scott and his friends gathered together, Tom went over to join the other parents to take photos. I loved seeing everyone laughing as they began their special night. The young men looked so grown up in their suits, and the young ladies were so beautiful in their colorful dresses.

During our "stakeout," I felt grateful to take part in this special time in Scott's life, even in just a small way. But after the photos were taken and we headed home, the reality hit me hard. "Tom, this is so difficult for me, always having to remain on the fringe and never being able to be with the people out there. I know I should feel happy, but I feel like crying."

I didn't get to go to Scott's graduation. Our family was well represented, though. As Tom and Scott's siblings headed out the door, they promised to take video and photos for me. I tried not to show my fragile emotions when saying good-bye and wishing Scott a great time of celebration. After everyone left the house I stood in the kitchen alone. I suddenly realized that moping around the house for the next number of hours was not a good idea, so I called my dear neighbor Julie, and she invited me right over. Together we watched a hilarious British comedy which helped take my mind off of what I was missing. Amid laughter and good tea with a close friend, the afternoon passed quickly and much less painfully.

As the weeks had now turned into months, I thought a lot about Job's physical problems while I dealt with my own. The book of Job says that he was given a terrible affliction of painful boils covering his entire body. He spoke of being glad that he had remained faithful to God while enduring unsparing pain. Job also spoke of his skin being covered with worms. We would call them maggots today. *Maggots. I've read that they could actually be beneficial in skin healing. Should I try such a strange therapy—maggots?*

Maggots love to dine on necrotic flesh. Job's skin, ruined by the boils, must have become horribly infected and died. Flies are attracted to such a treat. Their eggs become maggots. I knew that maggots can be our friends when they eat our dead skin. As they chomp away at the bad stuff, the healthy skin is able to grow.

I googled "maggot treatments" online and was surprised to discover that there were wound-care clinics that use maggots in virtually every U.S. state. Interesting. I was surprised and pleased that there were a few such clinics in Texas. So I called one of the maggot-treatment facilities. "Hi, do you really use maggots at your clinic?"

The nurse who answered heralded their use of maggots.

"Yes, we do use maggots as a treatment. They can be a truly wonderful answer for many people who have difficult wounds."

As I explained my facial condition, she asked, "Do you think your skin is dead?"

"No," I replied, "I think it is just infected."

"I'm sorry, but I don't think this is the right treatment for you. I don't think the maggots would be interested in your skin." Yet she continued to praise the wonders of maggots.

The next week, when I told Dr. Joy about my new maggot idea, she laughed. "Kristi, if you want us to use maggots, I'm off your case."

As I was seeking answers, I also spoke with one of Leaza's friends who was studying to be a nurse. "There's a new aid for stubborn staph infections," she told me. "It's a special honey called Manuka honey from New Zealand." I researched this honey online and printed off the information. When I showed Dr. Palik my research on the marvels of Manuka honey the following week, he questioned it as a viable option, but said that he would check it out.

Surprisingly, a few weeks later at a routine appointment, he said, "I actually asked one of the wound care nurses about Manuka honey. And guess what? The nurse I talked with was really excited about it. She said that her clinic was now using specialized bandaging with Manuka honey as an ingredient. She said it has brought effective healing for some of their most difficult cases."

I ordered a jar, but when I received it I could not figure out how to put the honey on my crusty face and still be able to remove it. The jar sat by my toaster for the longest time, but I just couldn't use it.

I was always searching for answers.

Chapter 18

Chamber of Horrors and Circle of Prayers

In late May, I once again saw Dr. Joy on a routine checkup. She looked at my face and promptly said, "Kristi we have not seen forward progress for the past few weeks, so I feel we need to try something new that might jumpstart the process." She explained. "Some people can benefit from hyperbaric oxygen therapy or HBOT. With the increased oxygen delivered to tissues, stubborn wounds and infections can heal more quickly." I was up for anything that might move my face condition forward.

I knew that HBOT infuses the environment with pure oxygen inside a pressurized chamber that people actually have to walk into. Just the thought of doing HBOT seemed intimidating, yet I met that week with the physician who had used it with various patients. He explained the process and it sounded like a good option. In preparation he noted, "When you come, wear only cotton clothing. Nothing should be on you that has metal or nylon. You will be putting a transparent globe over your head." I asked him how to keep my hair back. "Find hair clips and hair bands that have no metal connectors. Don't wear any fragrance, deodorant, or hairspray, either. The fumes might ignite in the highly oxygenated environment."

I must have looked concerned because he added, "Now, don't worry. You will be checked thoroughly when you come in because we want you and the entire group to be safe."

⟋⟍

On the morning of the first treatment, I was escorted to a women's locker room. While changing out of my street clothes and into their cotton smocks and footies, I read a chart displaying HBOT's positive effects, which helped to quell my inner trepidation. A staff woman came in and questioned me and verified that I had followed all the instructions completely. Together, we went to a large room where I sat and waited for the rest of the group to arrive.

When it was time for the treatment, a medical assistant came up to me and tried to place a white plastic ring and clear globe over my head. It was especially difficult for him to get the globe over the crusting sticking out of my forehead. I told him to be careful. When he finally succeeded, I felt like an astronaut. The whole environment felt a bit "out of this world."

As our group waited, I noticed four, fit-looking men sitting in front of long tables directly across from the huge blue windowless chamber, each working on his computer. Clean shaven with short hair, wearing matching navy blue, tight-fitting, Air Force-style jump suits with patches on their chests and sleeves, they looked like mission control for a space adventure. We were informed that their suits were made out of fire-retardant material. Good for them, but not comforting for me. Eight other patients and I were led toward the giant blue chamber, about ten feet wide and twenty feet long, just like a space crew approaching their capsule.

My fears increased as I walked into the chamber and sat down in the row of seats facing a wall-sized screen. A physician, also in a blue jumpsuit, wheeled in another man lying on a gurney who was hooked up to an IV. This doctor was apparently in charge of our group, and he gave us a choice of movies to watch. I was so glad when our group chose *Father of the Bride* and not one of the action films where things blow up.

Once the heavy door was closed, our fearless leader explained, "As this chamber becomes highly oxygenated and then returns to normal, expect changes in air pressure and heat throughout the process."

I tried to engage with the movie despite feeling claustrophobic and alarmed. Between all of us looking like astronauts with our globes on our heads and being shut off from the world, it was impossible not to think how bizarre this situation was. As the air pressure in the chamber changed, it became quite warm inside. At one point, I caught a glimpse of our doctor fiddling with some duct tape. I winced when he tore off a piece. *Couldn't static electricity start a fire?*

After about forty-five minutes we experienced more weird sensations as the oxygen levels and pressure gradually returned to normal. I don't think I've ever felt so relieved as I did when I could finally escape that chamber. As we departed, I asked the doctor who had been with us, "How often do you do this?"

He casually replied, "Anywhere from four to seven times a day."

Wow. I both admired him and wondered how he could do it sanely. Nerves of steel. To me, the whole process and experience felt very creepy.

When I saw Dr. Joy for follow-up, I explained that I just couldn't do the recommended ten-plus treatments of HBOT. She said, "I understand," but I knew she had hoped this would help me heal more quickly. That first HBOT treatment would be my last. As she studied my face, she added, "Kristi, you need to wash your face a bit more. Your moisturizer is building up too much on your skin."

⟆

In June, some dear friends from our home group told Tom and me that they had arranged for our pastor and an assistant pastor to come to our next Sunday evening meeting. "We want it to be a time of prayer to focus on the healing of Kristi's face." So thoughtful. I felt privileged and humbled.

Our home group was comprised of about ten couples. We happened to have joined them about a year earlier, and

I felt they were such a godsend. How fun and alive they all were. Involved with our careers, interests, and families, we talked and prayed as we enjoyed delicious food together. I looked forward to those Sunday nights.

At six o'clock the following Sunday, Tom and I arrived at a lovely upscale home and ate some dessert in the kitchen area. I felt embarrassed when the pastors came in and saw my damaged face. "Sorry for how I look," I apologized.

When it was time to pray, we gathered in the living room. Sunshine poured in through the windows as everyone scooted their chairs closer to me. Some stood nearby and placed their hands on my shoulders. After our pastor sat down across from me he asked several questions. "Kristi, do you know whether there are any areas of your life that need confession?"

I responded, "I've thought seriously about my sins over the past few months. I don't feel there is anything at this point that I have not already presented and confessed to God."

He then asked, "Do you have any special concerns?"

"One of the hardest aspects throughout this whole trial has been that God has felt very far away. I pray to him a lot, but he seems intangible, so distant."

The time of prayer began. Most of the men and women prayed for my healing. My friend Shelly prayed that if there was any spiritual warfare going on, our Lord would reign and defeat the enemy. I felt deeply touched by the abundant and diverse prayers offered on my behalf.

I was surprised when our pastor began to pray, "Lord, we pray for Kristi's inward soul, where she has also been wounded. This must be so hard for her as a woman to have a damaged face."

How did he know? It dawned on me for the very first time—*my face becoming so ugly had profoundly impacted how I felt as a woman.* This was a new insight for me. *Yes, my exterior wounds had impacted how I felt about myself on a deep level.*

Then he prayed, "Lord, may Kristi sense a fresh closeness to you."

As I sat in the middle of this caring and praying group of people, I anticipated with hope that the scales imbedded in my face would jump off my skin and fall into my lap.

I had a momentary flashback to a time very long ago, when I was a young teen listening to a reel-to-reel audiotape in our home. It was the true story of a Chinese Christian man who had been cruelly beaten for his faith. This particular man explained that during his days of torture by the communist police (using bamboo sticks under his fingernails), he noticed that one of the officials in charge had a malady where a scaly film seemed to cover part of his eyes. The Christian man offered to pray for the healing of his torturer. The official agreed. As the godly man prayed, the scales on the official's eyes instantly fell off! Not only was his act very Christ-like, praying for a persecutor with compassion, but he was also demonstrating to his accuser that God was truly in charge of this world. After the healing of the official's eyes, his persecution stopped.

However, on this night as we gathered in the living room in Dallas, nothing physically miraculous occurred. I opened my eyes as people compassionately prayed. There were no scales that fell off my face and into my lap. Yet, as the women and men continued to pray for me, I felt refreshed and ministered to on so many levels. The prayer time concluded.

Even now as I reflect on that evening in June, it remains one of my fondest spiritual memories—the living church reaching out with compassion—pastors, dear friends, and my husband all praying for my healing. So powerful to be loved so deeply. I did sense more of God's presence after that evening.

Chapter 19

Small Excursions and Sorry Comforters

Throughout this ordeal I had to take pleasure in simple things.

Oddly enough, baths became a great highlight to any day. Because my life was limited to doctor's offices, Tom's office, and our Sunday evening home group, taking a bath felt like an excursion from my very small world. Resting in the bubbles, I enjoyed total relaxation. I was content singing my little choruses to God. "Bless the Lord, Oh my soul, and all that is within me bless his holy name." When particularly discouraged, I might sing a Kelly Willard chorus that had brought me comfort during some of the dark days years ago when we lived in Budapest. She sings about casting our cares and laying all of our burdens down at Jesus' feet when we don't know what to do. That's exactly how I felt and what I needed to do every day.

Although a bath was refreshing, washing my hair felt like a magic trick worthy of Houdini. I would have loved to go to a hair salon each week, lean back in a chair, and have someone else wash my hair for me. That wasn't going to happen. I'd been told not to let any water get on the encrusted parts of my face, so I had to be extra careful. My new reality meant that I would first turn on the water in our tub, slide on my back with shampoo in hand, and ever so slowly raise my head toward the faucet to wet my hair, rub in the shampoo, and then wash it out—all done without hitting my face on the spigot. Not so easy.

It was emotionally hard to get out of the bath and see myself in the large mirror. There I was. My entire body looked normal while attached to my neck was this frightening head of mine. It was unsettling to see my disfigured face contrasted with the rest of my healthy self.

꒰ꄱ꒱

As I stood in the bathroom one evening, anticipating a hot, bubbly bath, suddenly a thought flew into my mind. *Kristi, you have been reading about Job's life, but you haven't blessed God yet as Job did. Why have I waited so long?* I knew I had prayed a lot to God during this trial with my face, and had thanked him for many answered prayers, but I had forgotten to bless God. It wasn't a matter of not wanting to bless him. It was a matter of not even thinking to do so. I think I was caught up in the trauma of my present trial.

So, I spoke out loud. "God, I'm so sorry that I haven't blessed you yet. I bless you tonight for being my God. I bless you for all you have done for me throughout my life. I bless you for giving me Tom, my family, and so many friends to encourage me and help me during this trial. I bless you as the God of the universe. And I bless your Holy name."

As I blessed God, I did not thank God for my face being in ruins with a staph infection that refused to leave. I didn't think God would even want me to do so. Jesus never told those he was healing to thank God for their sicknesses, demonic attacks, or the deaths of their loved ones. Instead, he understood that they were being afflicted, and he became deeply moved with compassion to touch, to heal, and to restore. Although I didn't thank God for my face being such an ugly diseased wreck, I could thank him for all the blessings he had given me during this time of suffering.

⁓

During one of my discouraging days, I received a gift from a dear friend in Dallas. Christine was a talented artist, and we have some of her paintings in our home. She knew I loved doing art and being creative.

So the package from Christine was a delightful treat. It contained a wonderful art related book and a packet of specialized ink pens. Her enclosed card included words of encouragement. "I hope you can enjoy creating while you are staying home." Such a thoughtful and personal gift—artist to artist. She included a small book, *The Art of the Soul,* by Joy Sawyer. It was comprised of meditations for the creative spirit, encouraging me to reflect the art within my own soul.

In the past, sometimes when I was stressed out I would paint to encourage myself. We have a watercolor framed in our kitchen that I did while we lived in Hungary. It shows a few flowerpots sitting on a window ledge. While we lived in Budapest, on many a Friday afternoon, I drove to the home of an artist friend, Melody, who lived outside the city. She and her family had come to Budapest for her husband's business, and we first met at the international church there. We soon became close friends as we did art together. On those lovely days, Melody would put on classical music, and we would spend the afternoon doing watercolors. Painting restored a sense of self while living in a foreign land and feeling so far from home.

However, during the many months of my facial ordeal, I felt so emotionally drained that I didn't have the energy to be creative. My passion for doing art would have to wait; I was in survival mode. I did use the pens from Christine to draw in my journal a bit, which had now become the place to express my heart and learning about the life of Job while on my journey.

⟨⟩

"Like one who takes off a garment on a cold day, or like vinegar on soda, is he who sings songs to a troubled heart." This proverb never rang truer to me than it did during this time.

One would think that listening to music would be a nice distraction and relaxing when I felt really stressed. For many people it is. But for me it seemed that most praise music was far too upbeat for my disturbed heart. Job expressed the same. "Therefore my harp is turned to mourning and my flute to the sound of those who weep." Job was not playing music as he wept in grief.

However, I discovered over time when our son Scott played songs on his guitar in his room in the evening, I felt more relaxed. Sometimes I would ask, "Scott, would you play a song or two for me?

"Sure, Mom."

So, his private, soothing music sessions took the edge off of my extreme inner stress and eased my suffering.

⌒⊙

Now, as I was dealing with a face that seemed to be stuck with a tenacious infection and not about to heal soon, I knew I needed ongoing, healthy human support. Throughout the long months I was ministered to by very wonderful, thoughtful, and tenderhearted comforters. I was actually pleasantly surprised that during my darkest days people would call or come by to encourage me. I felt safe in my relationships, even as I struggled.

I discovered that Job was not so fortunate. Three of his closest friends commiserated with him well at first and then turned on him. As I read the book of Job, I felt sad that Job had such miserable, cruel friends. Each one wielded a sharp pair of scissors, clipping at his heart by going after him with accusation after accusation. Their words were horrid. But they had started out so well.

The three men each assumed Job's suffering was clearly due to his sin. They admonished Job, "Figure out your sin, get righteous again, and God will restore you, you wicked man." They didn't know Job was declared by God to be the most blameless man on earth, and was afflicted "without cause." Chapter after chapter, the men made false assumptions. "If only you would repent of your sinful ways." Job called his supposed friends, "Sorry comforters."

⟟

There was only one time when I felt like I was dealing with a sorry comforter. One afternoon in June, I got a phone call.

"Hi, this is Candice. Can I come over on Saturday? I'd love to catch up."

"Sure. That would be great!"

Candice was a casual friend who I knew from teaching years ago. On Saturday, after we chatted a bit, I soon realized that this friend had an agenda. Smiling warmly she said, "Kristi, I think you need to consider if your face isn't healing at all, it's because you have sinned. Surely by now, after so many months and so many of us praying, you should be healed. What sins have you not repented of?"

I always feel confused when someone is smiling at me while they are accusing me of something. *Has she not read the book of Job? She sounds exactly like one of his miserable comforters.*

I wanted to question her, *"Don't you remember how furious God became with the three men for making incorrect assumptions about Job? They too were sure that Job's severe losses and boils were due to his sins. Not all suffering is due to someone sinning."*

But I didn't say what I was thinking. It didn't seem appropriate. I simply responded, "You know, early on in this process of losing my face, I spent a lot of time looking at my life deeply. I did look at the areas of sin in my life. I confessed all the sins I could think of. I asked God to show me places of sin I was not aware of. And I've tried to keep a short account with God. I can't think of any sins or patterns of sins I still need to confess."

"Well, you might need to still consider if your sins are the cause."

After my friend left that afternoon in June, I didn't think my words would have convinced her to change her opinion. But that didn't matter. What mattered was that God knew my heart, and I would keep my life open and transparent to him.

I was glad this friend stayed only a short while.

⌁

In many ways the book of Job is a living polemic against the dogma that blessings come only to the righteous and afflictions come only to the wicked. God graciously gives to those who don't deserve it. Meanwhile, many of God's righteous people suffer woefully, profanely, and deeply. Job had lived his life with remarkable integrity, helping out the widow, the orphan, the servant, and the most vulnerable. God declared twice that Job was the most righteous man on earth. Job was actually suffering "without cause" for months and was still remaining faithful to God. Enduring months of excruciating pain did not stop his loyal commitment to God, thus proving the depth of Job's integrity. Yes, Job complained and pleaded a whole lot. Yet, he was sure through his long endurance of suffering, "I will become like refined gold."

At the end of the book of Job, God at last goes after Job's three "not so great friends" as he stands up for Job. He had heard every one of their cruel accusations spouted at Job throughout the days, weeks, and months. And God's anger had been growing.

"It came about after the Lord had spoken these words to Job, that the Lord said to Eliphaz the Temanite, 'My wrath is kindled against you and against your two friends, because you have not spoken of Me what is right as My servant Job has.'" He went on, "Now therefore, take for yourselves seven bulls and seven rams, and go to My servant Job, and offer up a burnt offering for yourselves, and My servant Job will pray for you. For I will accept him so that I may not do with you *according to your* folly, because you have not spoken of Me what is right, as My servant Job has."

These three men had to face God's fury for their false assumptions that were "full of folly." But they had been so sure that Job's sin was the reason for his suffering. What Job had been saying about God and his suffering had been right all along. Only seven bulls and seven rams would suffice.

Yes, it is true that there are times when our suffering is due to God's discipline. But this was not true in Job's case. I don't know why, but I have often thought it best not to conjecture why someone is given great bounty in life, or why someone endures deep suffering. God only knows. That's what the book of Job is saying. He makes it clear that Job was not going through his time of severe testing due to sin.

But Job's friends, family, and community had been convinced otherwise. They were absolutely wrong. In the end Job's three primary accusers, in order to get Job's acceptance and God's forgiveness, were required to go to Job to make sacrifices for their sins. Additionally, each person in Job's family and community (who had all turned their backs on him) kindly and most likely humbly brought Job a coin and a ring of gold. They now consoled and comforted Job for all of his adversities.

I was grateful to experience only one "sorry comforter."

Chapter 20

∼

Burn Doctor

The good news was that the current antibiotic had stopped the progress of my staph infection. The bad news was that my face sat for the next number of weeks with absolutely no change, whatsoever. I racked my brain as to what to do to get out of this limbo.

My lasered face was basically a burn that had been complicated by an infection. *I know, I'll call a hospital that deals with burns. Perhaps a burn doctor there can help my face to finally heal. But would such a doctor be willing to try?*

When I phoned an area hospital that specialized in burns, the admitting nurse said she would talk to some doctors and get back to me. Two days later she called back with the name of a burn doctor who was willing to see me. I set up an appointment for the following Monday.

In the meantime, I was still traveling with Tom everywhere as the regimen of antibiotics once again caused difficulty in breathing which made me fearful of being alone. On Sunday morning, as I sat in the car while Tom went to church, I looked at my face in my makeup mirror. *Oh no. Oh no. There it is again. Yellow-gold fluid is coming out of a few new places on my face. But I've been so careful.*

When Tom returned to the car, I asked what he thought. He agreed that it looked like staph was popping up again. I had been on the mild antibiotic for many weeks now. The staph infection was mounting an attack. It was not willing to give up.

In a panic, I called Dr. Palik's office from my cell phone to seek his advice, but I couldn't get through to anyone on his answering service. All I could do was leave a message. I was so glad that I had an appointment with the burn doctor the following day.

On Monday afternoon, when Tom and I arrived to the burn hospital waiting room, we sat with people who were bandaged over various parts of their bodies. My heart went out to all of them. I could see their pain and also the concern of their companions and spouses. One man had a large bandage around his right hand. He looked despondent, but sat patiently with a woman who I assumed was his wife. The mood was stifling quiet and somber.

After Tom and I were escorted to a small room, a tall, dark-haired doctor strode in and introduced himself as Dr. Edward Drake. I gave him a quick synopsis of what had happened. Immediately, he put on his thick glasses, swung over on a rolling stool to where I was sitting, and peered directly into my face.

"Your face is scarred, you know."

Such an abrupt pronouncement startled me. I felt like bursting into tears. As he talked about the skin healing process using medical jargon—about fibroblasts and their function in skin recovery—my head felt it was in a fog. *What is he talking about?* I wanted to stop the conversation to let it all sink in. *I would be scarred.* I wanted to talk with Tom about how devastating this news was but now was not the time. If only I could just pack up and leave.

Of course I would be scarred. My face had been infected for weeks and imbedded with crusting. This is a logical assessment. Lately none of my doctors had addressed this issue because they were just trying to get my face to heal. I need to concentrate. I'm glad that Tom is here to listen and take notes.

Dr. Drake then pinched my skin, pulling off a clump of moisturizer. "You have too much lotion sitting on your skin. I think you are so fearful of washing your face that it is clogging it up so your skin can't heal. I suggest that you try washing it more thoroughly."

That was the same suggestion Dr. Joy had recently made.

He continued, "You have been on the current antibiotic for so long that it would be wise to change to a new one. I will prescribe the antibiotic Zyvox."

I quickly wondered if Zyvox was the antibiotic that Dr. Palik had wanted to wait to use until the very end because of its high potency. But I thought it made sense to try it now. *Maybe if I went on this new antibiotic and also washed my face more, I would be safe from infection. Perhaps my skin would finally heal.*

"You will have to have blood work done every week because Zyvox can damage the liver." Since his office was far from our home, he suggested that Dr. Palik's medical facility could do the blood work testing for me. He would contact him directly.

When I got home, I tried to reach Dr. Palik's office once more but couldn't get through to anyone. So, I began taking Zyvox with mixed emotions.

Dr. Palik finally called me a few days later. He had been on vacation. He was quite concerned about me taking Zyvox. Yes, he had wanted to keep that antibiotic in the arsenal down the line, and use it only if necessary. It was too late, though. I had been taking this potent medication, "the howitzer of antibiotics," as Tom called it, for five days. After the phone call all I wanted to do was cry. *Why do I feel like I never know what is right? One doctor says to do one thing, and another says to do something else. I feel like a yo-yo, unsure of which way will be best. Had I made a wrong choice?*

Chapter 21

Fateful Decision

Soon after, our oldest son Jon flew in from California for the weekend to visit us. He and his wife lived in Burbank, just down the road from where Jay Leno's *Tonight Show* was produced, and not too far from other studios. He was quite busy working in the film industry, so it meant so much that he would come to visit me.

Mom also happened to fly in to see me that same weekend. A double blessing. When we picked her up from the airport, she got into the back seat and studied my face. "Your face doesn't look as bad as I had expected." That was kind of her to say.

"How are you doing, Mom?"

"I'm feeling well considering everything. I'm trying some new alternative treatments for my cancer."

I was so grateful to have her with me as we were both battling dangerous health issues.

On Saturday Tom, Mom, Jon, Scott, and I all decided to visit Leaza, who was working that summer at a camp in East Texas. I was glad that during these past months she had been away at school and now at camp as I dealt with my facial issues. She is very empathetic, and I did not want her to be too negatively affected by my ups and mostly downs.

Just getting away from my normal regimen was a delight. I loved watching the beautiful pine woods go by as we drove through the east Texas countryside.

Parking at the edge of the camp by the lake, I looked up to see the blue sky full of white puffy clouds overhead. I breathed in the scent of pine trees and fresh air, so refreshing and freeing. Leaza soon greeted us. What a delight for all of us to catch up with one another.

At lunchtime, I stayed back in Leaza's cabin while everyone went to eat at the main dining hall. While looking out to the peaceful lake, I mulled over what do about the build-up of moisturizer on my face. I thought about how both Dr. Joy and Dr. Drake had noted that I needed to do something about it.

I began to come up with a plan. *Perhaps if I try gently rubbing off the moisturizer that's accumulating on my face, it will help my skin heal. But how would I do that with all the crusting stuck in my skin? That won't work. Plus, I don't want to spread the infection and hurt myself worse like what happened before. Maybe if I try standing in the shower the steam will soften off the crusting. Yes, that might be a good option.*

When everyone came back from lunch, I switched gears as we talked about different aspects of our lives. But my plan had taken shape in my mind.

Returning home late that afternoon, I decided "now was the time." Armed with the powerful Zyvox, I turned on the shower with warm water. As steam filled the room, I decided I would step into the back of the shower and let the mist soften the crusting. *It couldn't hurt, right?*

As I cautiously stepped into the tub, I stayed far from the shower head. Sure enough, with the misting my crusting quickly softened and fell off. As I watched the brownish looking stuff wash down the drain, I felt encouraged. My plan seemed to be working!

I got out of the shower, and as soon as I looked into our large bathroom mirror my optimism turned into horror. My face was not happy. Apparently my skin could not hold on normally. Most of my face looked dangerously exposed, red, and angry.

Clean but despondent, I rejoined my family downstairs. I sat next to Mom on the sofa in utter despair. I explained to everyone what I had just done. Tom, Mom, and Jon were so kind not to reprimand me, but I could see the concern on all of their faces. What I'd done had not been a good idea.

I sat in silence, feeling utterly devastated. I didn't know how they held their tongues from saying something about my lack of wisdom. I knew if they had said anything, I couldn't have handled it well. What was apparent to all was that I had been far too aggressive with my skin and had now created a major setback. I sat, shattered and furious with myself.

⁓

Sadly, both Jon and Mom needed to leave the following day. Tom drove Mom in for her early morning flight. Later that morning, I rode with Jon as we headed to the airport. Drizzling all morning long, the clouds finally burst, turning the rain into a blinding Texas downpour. As I sat in silence in the back seat, the windshield wipers flew a mile a minute, unable to keep up with the volumes of water cascading down the glass.

I couldn't speak.

Pelting mercilessly, the pounding rain reflected my brooding feelings and the reality of my circumstances. Grieving and feeling utter despair, I came to a conclusion. *Nothing is ever going to help my face, and I've just made it ten times worse.*

After I said good-bye to Jonathan at the airport, I got into the front seat and then drove home in the rain, as I wept inside.

I called the burn doctor the first thing Monday morning and was able to get an appointment with him the following day. As I showed Dr. Drake how my efforts to get rid of the moisturizer imbedded in my skin did not go so well, he didn't say much. Yes, the moisturizer was now gone. But what was left of my skin was severely damaged.

The attending nurse explained, "It's not best to try to treat staph by disturbing it. Debridement does not work in this case." I wish she could have helped with the healing of my face, but she made no offer.

As I began to walk out of his office, Dr. Drake explained that he could not really help me as he had hoped, but he offered to help me later. "Kristi, when you get all of the crusting off of your face, I want you to come back so I can fit you with a plastic mask. That way, as your skin heals, there will be less of a chance for it to build up the thick keloid scars that come from burns."

I went home feeling worse than ever. *By trying to follow the doctor's recommendations, I have done damage that I can never undo. I've made such a foolish decision.*

I had never felt such pervasive depression. Tom and I prayed together, asking God to show us what to do. We both felt overwhelmed by the seriousness of the setback, and this one was brought on by myself.

⌒

When I saw Dr. Joy later that week, she admitted that my face was a true mess. She was kind to me, but I could tell she was upset with me for removing my fragile skin. "You were not supposed to do debridement."

She also said that she had spoken earlier that day with my infectious disease doctor, Dr. Palik, and he told her, "I don't want to work with Kristi any longer as she is trying to go down too many directions at once." *Wow. That's devastating to hear. Would he ever be willing to see me again?*

I understood to some degree how Dr. Palik felt, but I was the only one living with the changes in my face, worrying, and searching for answers in this nightmare with no apparent solution. I hoped he would not give up on me altogether. I decided not to contact him for a while.

As we drove back home, Tom tried to encourage me, but I felt buried in sorrow and hopelessness.

Chapter 22

"Where Are You in My Darkness?"

With my face a terrible-looking mess due to my unwise action, I didn't want to see anyone. All I wanted to do was to climb into a dark hole and just sit alone in my misery at home.

"Tom, I'm not going to the office any more. When the people see what I did to my face and how dumb I was, well . . . I just can't go."

Midmorning, I got a call from Tom. "A few of the staff women are coming over for lunch. They wondered why you didn't come in today, and they want to see you."

"Okay. They can come."

Hearing of my weekend disaster, three of my dear friends from the office soon arrived, bringing deli sandwiches and flowers. We didn't even talk about my face. We just had fun talking as women do. They were able to draw me out of my doldrums, so by the time lunch was over I felt ready to move forward again. These three kind souls were a welcome lift to my broken self.

On the following day, I mustered up all my bravery and went back with Tom to the office, willing to face everyone. The office staff accepted me just as I was.

I continued taking Zyvox while faithfully having blood work done. So far it had not damaged my liver. Tom sometimes joked about the antibiotic saying in a robotic voice, "Kristi is taking, Zyvox from the planet Zycor." I appreciated his strange sense of humor.

Later that same week, as Tom and I arrived home from the office, we discovered a huge box on our front porch. What could it be? The enclosed letter read, "Kristi, we want you to have protection while you are out. We hope these visors will be helpful." Inside were several colorful visors. Some were pastel and some had cute patterns. The visors were from an office team of women in southern California who had been friends of ours for more than twenty years. I had never even thought there was both a practical and cute way to go out and be protected. I felt very touched at how these women were really looking out for me. Their unique and practical gifts brought joy in the midst of my storm.

◇

On Sunday, Tom and I were once again meeting with our home group, this time at a lovely home surrounded by beautiful old trees. It took extra courage for me to get out of the car and walk up to the house. *What am I to tell these friends who have walked with me for so long when they see my face looking like an angry mess, worse than it had before?* I finally gave a big sigh and walked in.

As soon as I saw my girlfriends gathered in the kitchen, I fell apart in tears. They quickly whisked me off into the master bedroom. As I sat on the bed, crying and voicing my discouragement, someone grabbed a box of tissues. Others sat down next to me or stood nearby. They didn't quote scriptures about how "all things work together for good," and they didn't offer quips like "Behind every cloud there is a silver lining." Instead, they listened and extended words of comfort. "We love you, Kristi. We are so sorry you have had more pain." Those words were exactly what I needed to hear. I had felt so defeated. After hugging me, the women and I joined the men for a delightful evening together. These friends were like Jesus who was deeply caring when he encountered people hurting from their many afflictions.

◯

Later that week, as I sat in the kitchen, feeling quite despondent about my damaged face, my dear aunt and uncle happened to call from Minnesota. They were my godparents and knew me quite well.

"How are you doing, Kristi?" I wanted to act like I was handling my facial setback with decorum, but I began crying. Choking back tears, I finally found my voice. As I explained the recent disaster with my face and how devastated I was for what I had done, they responded with deep empathy and acceptance. "We know you have been trying to find answers. We're so very sorry you are going through this."

This aunt and uncle understood profound suffering. Years ago, when one of their sons was only twenty-eight years old, he was diagnosed with brain cancer. My aunt had described to me how they were able to be with him during the latter stages of his illness when he wanted to be baptized. Caring friends were present to celebrate the joyous event of his baptism in a bathtub. My aunt spoke of her distress to see her dear son's body having become so lumpy from the metastasizing cancer. Despite all the promises from people in his church, some even telling them, "God has told us that your son with be physically healed," their beloved son died.

My dear aunt admitted to me a few years ago her deeply personal struggle. "When we lost our son, I experienced the greatest suffering I ever had experienced. And for the first time in my life God seemed intangible, like a vapor. Although I had walked with him for so long, I couldn't sense him at all."

My aunt wrote this poem:

WAS THAT YOU LORD?
(After the death of a son)

by Kris Lamp

When I felt no holy presence –
It was gone,
When I felt no stirring of God's love –

Only sadness,
When I felt no comfort –
Merely emptiness,
When I felt no reassurance from the One
I had come to know so well,
I thought I had been deserted and discarded,
And that special relationship with My Friend
Had somehow totally evaporated,
And things would never be the same.

But then I began to remember …

When I felt the strength and warmth of an arm
That hugged my shoulder,
Was that You, Lord?
When I saw a pair of eyes well up with tears
Knowing my sorrow,
Were those Your eyes, Lord?
When a hand clasped mine
And squeezed it in sympathy,
Was that Your hand, Lord?
When my loved ones gathered into a ring,
With arms interlocked in love,
Were You there, too, Lord?

Now I know that it was You, O Lord,
And you had been there with me all along.
Yes, that was You.

I learned from my aunt that sometimes God's presence seems ungraspable when we need him the most. But this idea of God distancing himself when we desperately need him violates our human expectations that we will always sense God more strongly and closely especially while suffering. I also realized that God often uses people to extend his caring presence to those who are experiencing pain and loss. We all need other people to come to us and alongside us to ease our broken-hearted pain, especially when God might feel so very far away. Each of us can be his tear-filled eyes, his comforting voice, and his tender touch.

That's what my aunt and uncle had become to me. Their timely, early evening call was the best medicine. I cried throughout most of our conversation on the phone. In the end they brought me the most soothing and truest of comfort through their empathetic voices. They somehow knew how to bring deep-reaching comfort to my soul.

Because neither keeping my face moisturized nor getting it too wet had worked out so well, I decided to quit putting anything on it altogether. *Maybe drying it out would help my skin heal in some way.* So I spent much of my day with a fan blowing on me. My face did begin to look a bit less messy as it dried up.

It was now early July and a few weeks after my "misting disaster event." With courage and trepidation, I decided to call Dr. Palik's office. *Whew.* Thankfully, he was willing to see me. When he examined my wounded face, he determined that the infected areas were stable, but there still was no actual improvement even while trying to dry it out. I seriously wondered whether I would ever have normal skin once again.

✒

When I traveled, always riding in the backseat of our car to avoid the sunlight, I marveled at others who were out and about.

Will I ever be out there going to where I want to go and when I want to go? Will I ever have that freedom? I wonder how other people who have been disfigured feel when they can't get out easily? How sad it must be for them. I guess they eventually find ways to adjust.

As I envied all the people scurrying around, living life so naturally and freely, I bemoaned my situation to Tom. "I don't want to be always hiding in the back seat, riding in the car like a dog."

Tom was quick to respond. "Just pretend you are so wealthy that you've hired me to be your private chauffeur."

From then on, I affectionately named Tom "François," my French driver. He even accommodated at times with a French accent. "Bonjour, Mademoiselle. Where would you like to go today? How about the park. It tis a beautiful day. Oui?" Tom could always make me smile.

✒

I never got used to the fitful and sleepless nights that had become a norm over the past months. And I sometimes lamented my lack of a good night's sleep. *Why should I even try to sleep tonight? I know, I'll go downstairs and try to rest there.* Our Scottish Terrier, Winston, often joined me as my faithful furry companion. Dogs really do come in handy sometimes.

One late summer night, giving up on trying to sleep, I decided to walk out to the backyard. Winston came trotting along. Together we sat down by the pool. I plopped my bare feet on the top step to feel the refreshing warm water on my toes. As Winston sat beside me, I rubbed his thick black fur. I looked up at the moon, feeling abysmally lonely.

There is something welcoming about the lights of the stars and moon hanging out there in the dark night sky for all of us to see. But on this humid night, the hazy moon seemed cold and lifeless. I yearned to sense God's presence once more.

I thought back to when "Mr. Moon" had brought me comfort while we lived overseas in Hungary. Longing to be back home in America, I had felt so isolated there. On many a night I gazed out the large back windows of our lovely Budapest home perched on the hill. The warm glow of the moon light cascaded through the glass and onto the parquet floor. Knowing that the moon I could see there in Budapest was the same moon I had always loved since my childhood in Texas made me feel safe.

The night skies often reminded me of my dad's love of the moon and stars. When growing up in Texas, Dad would take us three girls out to our backyard to show us the various constellations. And ever since those days, God seemed nearer when I looked at the night sky. But not tonight. The moon seemed sad and lonely too.

"God are you there?"

The silence seemed deafening.

Mournful, I looked back to the moon once again as I walked back into the house. I reminded myself that God was surely watching, even when he seemed so distant and intangible.

ᜒ

I was beginning to learn that God is as sovereign in his silence as he is when he makes himself known. I had not often experienced God's close presence during this wilderness time. Nor did I always experience a peace "that passed all understanding." I had a sense this time of trial was where God had placed me, and that was something I would accept.

Job also spoke during his months of misery of not being able to find God. At other times, he felt that God was attacking him like a warrior, and he wished God would leave him alone. I decided that whether I sensed God's strong comforting presence during this time or not, I wanted to be like Job and continue to talk with God honestly and to trust and reach out to him no matter what.

But it wasn't easy.

Chapter 23

⌒

Top Doc, and a Scary Face

It was now mid July. One of the doctors who was part of our home group came up to me on Sunday. After looking closely at my face and noticing no improvement, he said, "Kristi, I personally know one of the top infectious disease doctors in Texas. I'm calling him this week to get you an appointment. He uses infusions of antibiotics."

This opportunity for expert help was encouraging. I didn't know what infusions were, but it sounded like a new direction that might lead to a solution.

Sure enough, an appointment was set up.

When Tom and I showed up to the crowded office later that week, I felt immediately embarrassed. Everyone in the waiting room looked perfectly healthy to me. Most patients were young, good looking, nicely dressed men and women. When I went to register, the receptionist just asked for me to speak my name. There was no sign-in sheet. As I turned around, I quickly decided not to sit down with the other patients.

Instead, I walked over to a large magazine rack in a corner of the room and turned my back to everyone so I wouldn't scare them. I grabbed a magazine and pretended to read a few articles.

When my name was called, Tom and I met with Dr. Ben Klein, the doctor with broad knowledge of very complicated infections. As he read through my records and looked at my face, I could tell he was trying to think of some conceivable way to help.

He became concerned when he heard that I had been taking Zyvox for a few weeks. He warned me, "I personally never prescribe it for more than a week, at the very most ten days."

I was way beyond that now, a potentially dangerous situation.

"Be sure to keep having your blood work done. I will see you in a few weeks to check on any changes, but at this point I have no recommendations. I first need to consult with Dr. Joy."

No recommendation at all? That was definitely not what I wanted to hear.

My hopes for starting a new regimen were temporarily dashed. We would have to wait once again for a possible solution.

⌒

The early weeks of searching for answers for my messed up face had now turned into five months since the initial procedure, and I still had no positive changes. It was becoming increasingly hard for me to drum up the courage to go to our home group at all. "Tom, I don't want to go tonight. I feel at a loss." Tom tried to help. "Kristi, you know that being with our friends will lift your spirits." I knew he was right.

Arriving at our host's home, a friend rushed up to me and said, "Let me see your face." She stared at my forehead. "Darn it. Nothing has changed. So sorry, Kristi."

My sentiments exactly.

I always managed to relax and feel safe in the presence of these friends as we met together to eat, to talk, and share our lives. However, on this particular evening, as the women gathered to share our prayer requests, I suddenly felt stuck. I was tired of asking for prayer. It just seemed selfish and pointless. *We all have prayed about my face infection for months. Nothing has changed. Why keep asking for prayer?*

When it came my turn to share, I merely said, "You all know my need. I don't feel like saying anything more tonight."

After the prayer time, one of my friends gently pulled me aside. Beth and her husband had endured a major loss several years ago when one of their children died due to a brain injury. She explained quietly, "Kristi, some people expected me to have moved forward a few months after our daughter's death, but I was not there. So when they asked, 'How are you doing?' I responded, 'I'm okay,' because that is what they wanted to hear."

Beth was encouraging me to hang in there. She also was kindly conveying that my current distress was acceptable and understandable to her. There would be times when

I felt that others wanted me to handle my trials according to their expectations and not my own reality. I could tell them I was okay and know that it was okay to not be okay.

⌀

One would think that enough was enough. But later on that week, while at Tom's office, my right eye became itchy. Assuming staph was now in my eye, I made an emergency appointment with my ophthalmologist. I talked with the receptionist over the phone, "I think I have an eye infection. My entire face is infected and I look really scary and don't want to frighten off your other patients. Do you happen to have a back door?"

"Yes, we do. Go on around back, and I'll meet you there."

When the eye doctor examined my eyes he determined that I had a staph infection in both of them. Not surprising. Now we had a new regimen. Tom would now need to administer eye drops twice a day, ensuring the medicine got to where it needed to go and didn't accidentally run down onto my face. It wasn't easy to sit still and lean back in a chair as Tom zeroed in with the eyedropper.

When I met with Dr. Palik later that week, he said, "I'm frankly surprised that you have not contracted an eye infection earlier. You have so much infected skin above your eyebrows. I'm also amazed after so many months that you don't have staph in your ears as well."

Seriously?

He checked out my ears and both were fine. At least I could be grateful for that.

Since things had recently been so tough, Tom thought I could use a change of scenery. He decided to treat me to a stay at a hotel near the camp where Leaza was working. Scott came along for the ride. Thankfully, by the time we picked up Leaza, the four of us arrived so late to the hotel that no one was around. I wore a baseball cap as we hurried up the elevator and into our room.

I woke up early Sunday morning to hear and see Leaza laughing and giggling in her sleep. Hilarious.

After she woke up, and we had a good laugh, she pronounced, "Mom, I'm tired of seeing you wearing the same tops over and over again. You need some variety. I'm going out to get you some new clothes. There's a Target nearby."

While she was gone, I looked through the sheer drapes of our hotel window and watched the people laughing, talking, and enjoying their lives around the pool. *Someday. Maybe someday I can be having fun out there where the people are.*

Leaza soon returned with several new tops—cute, colorful ones that were perfect for me. Buttoned or zippered tops had become my only option for safety's sake. If a shirt had a collar, I would fold it under so as not to accidentally brush my cheeks. The fun of having new clothes, because I hadn't been able to get out and shop for months, brought wonderful refreshment to my regimented life.

When it was time to leave the hotel, Tom got permission from the front desk for us to use the service elevator. It was kind of fun sneaking out the back way and walking through corridors that only the hotel staff used. We all felt a bit clandestine.

⟡

No matter where I was, reactions to my distorted face were to be expected. Once, when I was standing in line at the burn clinic waiting to pay my bill, a little girl about age five looked up and saw me. Despite the visor that covered my forehead (the most disgusting part of my face) she yanked on her mother's pants and said, "Mommy, Mommy, look at that lady."

Her mother responded, "Honey, it's not polite to stare at people."

The girl became even more insistent, pulling on her mom's pants more vigorously. "No, Mommy, you really have got to look at that lady!"

So the young mom glanced at me briefly and turned back to her daughter. "That lady probably has a burned face." If only she knew the reality.

Getting on elevators was also interesting. Some people simply would not get on with me and chose to wait for the next one. Those who ventured into the elevator sometimes stood in a far corner opposite to where I was standing. Medical personnel stared at my face, trying to figure out what malady I possibly had. I did not blame people for their natural reactions.

Often in waiting rooms people avoided sitting in the open seats next to me, evidently fearing they might catch what I had. One day, while waiting in a very packed room at a hospital, a woman sat down next to me. When she looked up and noticed my face for the first time, she quickly scooted her entire body as far away from me as she possibly could. I did not feel slighted at all. I would have done the same thing.

On another day on the way to work, Tom dropped by an auto repair shop to have our car evaluated. A friendly mechanic came out and reached his hand through the open driver's side window to greet Tom. As he put his hand through the window again to greet me in the back seat, Tom casually said to him, "Don't worry. She just has a staph infection." As soon as he saw my face, he yanked his hand back as if it was on fire. I was amused that he could maintain his friendly demeanor afterwards.

So, I never felt offended by anyone's natural reaction to seeing my face. Sometimes I actually found it a bit humorous. I scared myself all the time just catching a glimpse of myself in a mirror.

Chapter 24

With a Potato Chip Face, I Began to Wonder...

I felt a distinct sense of loneliness during the process of trying to find an answer. At my older sister's urging, I sent off a large packet of my health records to her renowned dermatologist near Los Angeles. Kari's doctor offered to try to treat me, if I could get to California. I didn't know how I could get there easily as flying was out of the question. Perhaps later.

Thankfully, Kari and her husband, a long-haul trucker, happened to be coming through Dallas in July on their way east, bringing along her two Schipperke dogs with them. Mind you, these are small, black, very rotund, and quite frisky dogs. As soon as they came into the house, they jumped all over our furniture, excited to see us and our Scottie.

Kari had been so very caring ever since she heard of my facial troubles, calling me several times each week to check up on my physical and emotional state, always listening, always empathizing. Now as we sat together in the family room she laughed. "Your face looks like it's covered with bits of potato chips in different colors that are sticking out in all directions." So true.

For two days, Tom and I were given the gift of diversion. It was hard to say good-bye as Kari and her husband drove away with her dogs perched up on the dashboard. *Would I ever have the freedom to be out "on the road again?" Would I someday live life no longer centered around my face?* I lived a strange life.

⌒

It was now late July and we would have to wait another week to meet with Dr. Klein. As the crusting remained embedded in my face, never budging, and my doctors seemed to be at a stalemate as to what to do, Tom was given the name of a highly recommended dermatologist at a major hospital who was willing to take a look.

With low expectations, we drove to the hospital to meet Dr. Wilson. As soon as I walked into his inner office, the doctor brought in a cluster of resident students. "Come in everyone. I want you to see this woman's condition." I felt like a specimen in a jar as each of the students came up one by one and studied my face closely. I felt embarrassed, and once again was reminded that my face was a textbook-worthy anomaly.

Then Dr. Wilson spoke to me in front of the students, "The answer is simple. You must soak your face twice daily in a solution. Come back in two weeks." I tried to tell him that getting my face wet in the past didn't work out so well. He wouldn't listen. *I know what's best for you seemed to be his attitude.* I left the office feeling humiliated and dismissed. As we headed out to the car, Tom said, "That doctor was pretty proud and rude, like one of the arrogant physicians depicted on *ER.*"

"Yes, I felt kind of de-humanized while I was there."

I called Dr. Joy and Dr. Palik to ask what they thought of his recommended protocol. They both strongly discouraged me from trying the soaking solution. I agreed, and cancelled my follow-up appointment. Another dead end.

Each month had become increasingly harder emotionally. I now cried about once a day just a little, using a tissue to dab the inner corners of my eyes. It was cathartic and a necessary outward spilling of the pain that came from within. I had become accustomed to my strange lifestyle—still using a straw to get most of my nourishment, spending the days at Tom's office, going to doctor's appointments, and being sequestered at home. I began to seriously wonder whether I might die someday if the staph infection that lived in my face became systemic.

During early August, Tom was out of town once again while my orange stuffed monkey kept me company. One afternoon I felt an inexplicable sensation, as if my body was shutting down. As I rested on our bed upstairs, it seemed like it would be so easy to give up, give in, slip away, and perish right then and there. Painless. I had never felt this way before.

This isn't good. I need to fight this.

I immediately got out of bed, went downstairs and sat on the love seat, and tried to rev up my tired and waning self. I drifted in and out of sleep. Feeling concerned, I got down on the floor and grabbed a deck of cards off the coffee table in order to play some solitaire. I could hardly turn the cards over. I quit. I got back up on the love seat to rest. *What's wrong with me? It must be the Zyvox. It's killing me.* I decided then and there not to take it anymore.

Tom called later that evening to check on me. "Are you lonely?"

"No, I'm too tired to be lonely. I felt so weak today that I had to crawl just to get from the love seat to the bathroom and back again. I have no energy to stand up. I've decided to quit taking the Zyvox." Tom agreed and asked me to keep him posted.

The following day a nurse called from Dr. Palik's office with great concern in her voice, "You need to stop taking Zyvox immediately. The lab report came back. Your liver function is being negatively affected." I had made a wise decision. This powerful drug was now off limits.

When Tom returned home, he became further concerned as he saw my continued sluggishness and discouragement, so he took me to see Dr. Joy. As we walked from the car to the office, I had to hang on him in order to keep walking. I lay down on the observation table while we waited for the doctor to come in. I felt utterly exhausted. Dr. Joy talked with us, and then she and Tom discussed whether I should consider taking an antidepressant. I tried to explain to them, "I'm not feeling depressed. I'm just so very tired."

As we left the office, Dr. Joy said, "If there aren't any positive changes, please let me know."

In a few days my energy level came back. Unfortunately, so did my infection.

Chapter 25

⨯◯

"Don't Come Back"

Mid-August had now arrived in Texas. Temperatures hovered around 100, and I hunkered down indoors. Within a week of stopping Zyvox, the left side of my face became increasingly painful. The pain grew so intense on Saturday night that I called a local hospital in the late hours. The nurse on call was very empathetic as I described my symptoms, but unfortunately she had no recommendations. I asked her whether she knew of any wound care clinics, and she kindly provided phone numbers for two local places. I thanked her and added, "I'll probably be coming in tomorrow."

Sure enough on Sunday morning, after a fitful night of sleep, I knew I needed medical help. The pain in my left cheek had intensified throughout the night. Tom took me to the local hospital, and we sat in a large, crowded waiting area. But not for long. We were quickly escorted into a private room, probably because my face was a bit frightening to the other patients.

A female doctor came in. As we discussed my condition, I could tell she was racking her brain as to what would be the best way to treat my face. "I'm going to have to physically remove the scabbing on the left side. It's fully infected." She pulled on some white latex gloves and grabbed some gauze from a lower drawer. She cautioned me, "This will hurt." She grabbed the crusting that was now removable and much of it fell into her hand while some of it flew onto the floor. She threw what she could into a bio-hazard receptacle and then placed the gauze directly into the wound.

Without a word, she made a speedy exit.

We waited a long while in the empty room, but the doctor never came back. I think she was freaked out by what she had just seen and done. Eventually, a young practitioner came in and announced we could go home. When I asked her how I should get the gauze out of the wound she offered, "Just soak it."

That would be easier said than done. At home, the gauze did not want to budge. I even lay that portion of my face in a bowl of water for about a minute, but the gauze remained embedded in my face. Then, I gritted my teeth and painstakingly began to pull it out of the wound, crying as I did so. When I finally got it all out, I lay down on our bed, completely exhausted, and waited for dinner.

When I woke up from a dead sleep, to my horror a clump of my hair had fallen across the open wound and was now stuck to it. *Will this ever end?*

I went downstairs in tears and showed the problem to Tom as he was cutting up some vegetables. He turned from what he was doing, looked me in the eyes and then quickly yanked my hair out of the wound. Blood flew across the floor and countertops as I screamed in pain. Problem solved.

Unfortunately, just then Leaza and our niece came in through the garage door together and heard me wailing. I did not want them to be traumatized further so I quickly ran back upstairs. Distraught by the awful day, I sat on the bed and poured out my soul to God with many tears.

⌒

I needed reinforcements. After hearing the latest news of my infected face, Mom became more concerned, sensing my deepened hopelessness from the recent setback. Although she was dealing with her own battle with cancer, she told me on the phone, "I'm coming out for a visit." I felt humbled and grateful.

This time Mom not only brought her presence but also some small silver candlesticks. She said she wanted to give them to me, knowing how much I liked family-related items. Her gifts made me wonder if she sensed that her battle with cancer was taking its toll, and this was perhaps a "good-bye" act of love. As the days went by, Mom polished each of those pieces until they gleamed. I took it as a reflection of her deep love for me.

Mom was a constant learner, and like me, she would not give up easily in finding solutions to a problem. She was always up on the latest news, interested in many areas open for discussion—including politics, interesting books she was reading, educational issues (she had a doctorate in education), and topics regarding faith. We had great conversations as she shared with me what she was learning. She definitely wanted to go with Tom and me when we went to see my doctors that coming week.

On Friday afternoon, Tom, Mom, and I visited Dr. Klein, the latest infectious disease specialist, for the second follow-up appointment. I was hopeful he would have some new insight and perhaps start specialized treatments, especially in light of my latest setback. I explained, "Having no Zyvox meant more infection. Do you have a suggestion?"

He simply pronounced, "I talked with Dr. Joy. I have no answers."

Surely, I wasn't hearing right.

Then he said, "I see no reason for you to come back."

I was shocked.

Really? Don't come back? What am I to do if one of the top infectious disease experts doesn't have any solutions? I didn't know what to say so I said nothing.

Tom tried to ask further if there was any other possible direction we should consider, such as getting an infusion of antibiotics. "Can you give us any suggestions at all?"

Dr. Klein shook his head. "No. Kristi has been on the strongest of antibiotics. Should she get an infection through an infusion, we would have nothing to stop it." Then he spoke to me directly, "Do not set up another appointment. I cannot help you. Keep on working with Dr. Joy."

Klein's absolute refusal to see me anymore staggered me. I had expected an infectious disease expert to be willing to try to solve my problem at least a little longer. Surely he had dealt with very complicated cases before. Yet, he thought he could not solve my case, so he would not try. I sadly paid my co-pay and left the office.

I felt somewhat abandoned, but not without hope. I had another appointment with Dr. Joy the following week. She always seemed to have new ideas, and she had been a great support to me emotionally.

ᴄᴑ

As Tom drove us to Dr. Joy's office on Monday morning, I told Mom, "I'm so glad you can meet the doctor who had been such a tremendous help since last March. She's amazing." After quick introductions, Dr. Joy looked at my face and then announced to all of us, "I have given some thought to your case. I have a new idea."

I eagerly anticipated her thoughts.

"Kristi, I honestly can't help you anymore. We basically have seen no changes over the past five and a half months. It's time for you to move on in another direction. Here's the name of an immunologist." She wrote the name of a doctor on a piece of paper and handed it to me. She then added, "Don't make another appointment."

What? This can't be happening! She, too?

Unbelievable. I felt like I had been hit by a freight train. I was shocked and shaken. Absolutely crushed. I mumbled something about how hard this would be if I could not see her anymore. Sharing my concern, Tom asked, "Can we at least call you for advice if we need a second opinion?"

"Yes, of course," she responded "I would be glad to help in that way."

Although she let me down as nicely as she could, it still didn't change the fact that I had been dumped by two doctors in a week's time. And both were outstanding in their fields. I couldn't even go back to either of their offices. Now, I was really adrift, all on my own.

After we left the office, I slumped into the back seat of our car. Overwhelmed with hopelessness and despair, I moaned, "What will we do now? I feel totally abandoned! Where do I turn? I know in my gut this is not an immunology issue. I can't believe this!"

Mom could not fully understand why I was so upset. Tom stopped the car in the parking lot as he tried to explain. "We are upset because Dr. Joy has been our mainstay since the beginning, way back in March. She has been our primary source of wisdom, help, and perspective. We saw her every few weeks throughout all these months. Now, that we can't come back, we have really no one to turn to. No one." Mom then understood how devastating this last blow was.

When we returned home, my pervasive hopelessness settled in, like a dark fog excluding everything else from sight. I decided I might always look like a monster and have to live the life of a recluse, as long as I could somehow keep this infection from killing me. I had looked like a crazy lady for so long. Now it seemed there would be no end.

⌒

Upstairs in our bedroom, I shared my fears with Tom privately. Standing in front of him, I pointed to my face. "What if I look like this for the rest of my life?"

As I searched his eyes, he put his hands on my shoulders and sweetly looked down at me. With the tenderest of expressions he responded, "I love you. And I will always love you if you look like this the rest of your life. When I married you Kristi, I married you for the whole package."

He kissed me on the top of the head. I felt so grateful to have the man I loved love me back in such a profound way, even with such a hideous face.

When I returned downstairs, I could hear Mom making phone calls from the living room. Apparently she had brought with her a list of top dermatologists from around the country and was calling their offices one by one. I could hear her pleading my case over the phone. She would ask, "Can't you possibly get her in earlier than six weeks from now?" Or, "Can't you find an opening? My daughter desperately needs your help. She could die from the staph infection."

Mama bear was fighting for her baby bear. Her caring endeavor meant so much to me, but after over an hour on the phone, Mom could not find even one doctor willing to take me earlier than six weeks away. I knew that she was now taking Vicodin twice a day to help control her own pain, so I was humbled that she was fighting for my health and life even while cancer was taking over her body. Mom, Tom, and I prayed for wisdom.

⌒

Feeling desperate, the next morning I decided to call the two wound care clinics that had been suggested by the late-night emergency room nurse.

Despite initial reluctance from each office, I was relieved to be able to set up appointments for the following week, one on Monday and another on Wednesday. At least they would take a look at my face.

Tom, Mom, and I arrived Monday afternoon to a wound care clinic that happened to be close by. Assigned to my case was a female doctor who kindly offered the only idea she could think of. "Put Silvadene ointment into the wounded area a few times a day."

It sounded totally impractical, but out of respect for her, I would at least give it a try. So when I returned home, I placed a dab on a small spot on my left cheek. Trying to remove the ointment the following day proved impossible. I asked Tom for help. He tried and decided we were just hurting my skin further.

Upon hearing of my latest setbacks, my sister Lauri decided to join us. "I'm flying to Dallas tomorrow." I could use all the reinforcements I could get.

She arrived on Tuesday evening. As we all sat at the kitchen table, we talked and laughed, and at times I cried while I tried to explain the saga of the past week. There's something comforting that only a caring family can bring. They knew me. They loved me. They had supported and prayed for me week after week. Now they came to help in any way possible.

I was grateful that I had the second wound-care clinic appointment the following day. One last try.

Chapter 26

"I Know What to Do"

When Wednesday morning arrived, Lauri drove Mom and me to the wound care clinic located at a large hospital. As we sat in the waiting room, we all felt the weight of how much rode on this appointment.

When I was brought back to the examination room I sat on the blue medical lounge chair, my legs dangling over the edge, waiting for the doctor to arrive. Mom was perched in a chair with a pad of paper and a pen, ready to take notes. I explained to Lauri who stood nearby, "After today's appointment, I have no options left here in Dallas. I can't think of even one new doctor to see. The only option is to get to California to see Kari's dermatologist. He said he'd be willing to try to help me, but I can't get on a plane. The airlines wouldn't let me fly with my face looking this way."

Sensing my desperation, Lauri said, "I'll drive you all the way to California myself if that's what we have to do."

I sat quietly and began to cry, my tears falling onto the linoleum floor. I felt utterly hopeless.

Soon a nurse entered. She wore blue scrubs, had a trendy haircut and a warm smile. She introduced herself as Jenny Ward. As she took control of the appointment, I couldn't help thinking, *I don't need a nurse. I need a doctor.*

Jenny studied my records, asked several questions, and looked closely at my face. She then asked, "Has anyone tried bandaging your face over the past few months?"

I answered, "No, not since the initial procedure."

Jenny went on to explain. "The crusting in your skin needs to be removed. Skin cannot grow over it or under it. It is fibrin and very hard."

I could easily agree. It felt like I had glass chips stuck in my face everywhere.

"I think I know what to do. We should try some specialized bandaging that can soften the crusting and soak up the leaking fluid so your skin can heal. I've seen a case similar to yours on a leg wound several years ago where I used this procedure. The bandaging must be changed every day. This method should work."

Every day? I could not believe my ears. Since March, I often felt stranded for days and weeks between appointments, wondering if anything was working or if something had gone terribly wrong. Now I felt hope! I would be seen every single day.

Jenny offered to take my case. "I'm astonished that no one has previously suggested this course of treatment over the past five and a half months." She described what the wound care treatment would specifically entail, and it sounded like an onerous journey for both of us. I couldn't believe she wanted to work with me until my face was healed.

Jenny said, "I'd like to get started this afternoon."

"I need to contact my primary doctors first, my infectious disease doctor and my dermatologist. In the past, sometimes treatments didn't go so well."

"Of course. Call the office when you find out."

Fortunately, I happened to have an appointment that afternoon with Dr. Palik because I wanted him to look at my re-wounded left side. So off we three went, Lauri, Mom, and I. We arrived at his office and assumed the same positions—I sitting on an exam table, Lauri standing to the side, and Mom sitting in a spare chair with her pen and paper, ready to be the scribe.

Dr. Palik arrived and listened to the summation of recent events and of nurse Jenny's recommendation. Thankfully, he concurred.

"This treatment makes sense, but have the nurse begin with a small trial area. You need to take a mild antibiotic during this process because your skin will be disturbed." He gave me a prescription.

As we left his office I immediately called Dr. Joy on my cell. She soon returned my call and agreed with Dr. Palik that a trial area would be the first step and possibly a good one.

Okay, great. Two thumbs up.

When we returned to the wound care clinic that afternoon, Jenny first took several pictures of each part of my face and measured the size of each wound area. The diagnosis in her records read, "complicated wound."

She then cleaned a section on the lower right side of my face (the least damaged area) and applied the specialized bandaging that included an antibiotic. "I normally do not treat faces," she said, "but I can see no reason why this bandage treatment would not work on a face. I will see you tomorrow at three o'clock. Be sure to take some pain meds."

∞

Arriving at the wound care clinic the following day felt like a major event. Tom took off work to join my mom and sis to witness the first unveiling. I sat quietly, my head resting against the sloped backrest of a wide blue vinyl exam lounger. Jenny came in with her supervising physician, Dr. Edwards. Both seemed filled with anticipation. As Jenny set up her medical materials, she explained that she had been in e-mail contact with Dr. Edwards the night before, sending him the info regarding my case. She wanted him to verify the effectiveness of the wound care treatment she was trying.

Jenny started the procedure by peeling the dressing away from my skin. Lauri and Tom grabbed my ankles, while Mom held onto my wrists to defer the pain from my face. After opening a clear pink canister of saline solution, Jenny began removing the bandage, carefully cleaning my wound with Q-tips. The pain was awful, but I would not cry. Not now. This was too important.

After about ten minutes Jenny finally said, "Let's take a look."

With wide eyes, like two children looking in the window of a candy store, Jenny and Dr. Edwards peered at my face through a large magnifying glass. Jenny exclaimed, "Look, the epithelial buds have come in!"

"What are those?" I asked.

"That's what your skin grows over. And look," she added. "The skin around the edges is already trying to grow inward. This is going to work!" She added, "The skin usually grows from the outer edges inward and sometimes creates little peninsulas and odd shapes as it does so."

Both medical experts were enthusiastic.

Jenny invited Mom, Lauri, and Tom to look at the wound, and they didn't seem to mind.

Tom stared. "It looks kind of like the edges of a lake as it is just beginning to freeze with a very thin layer of ice."

Jenny handed me a mirror and asked if I wanted to see the wound as well.

"Oh, no," I said. "I could never!"

Jenny and Dr. Edwards talked about where and how I should best be treated. After some discussion, they decided I definitely should not be treated at the hospital. Both were concerned about me picking up another infection.

"If you get a MRSA that would be quite dangerous because you have been on so many antibiotics already." They determined that I should come to the clinic three times a week, and nurses would visit me at home on the other days. Jenny offered to begin the initial treatments herself to ensure the best start.

As we wondered what to do on the days I did not come to the clinic, she asked where I lived. We were excited to discover that we lived about twenty minutes apart.

"You live so close, I can treat you at your home this Saturday and Sunday. Your house is between my home and the clinic. I'll just stop in on my way to work."

Amazing! Here Tom and I live in this giant metroplex, and Jenny lived so close by. We had traveled to so many medical facilities both near and far, and perhaps now the solution was only twenty minutes away.

Tom and I rejoiced with Lauri and Mom that night. Together we thanked God that we might have finally found the answer that we had been searching and praying for for so long.

On Friday, Lauri, Mom, and I returned for my next treatment at the clinic. As Jenny set up her supplies, she placed on the counter a green plastic bag from The Body Shop and said, "I think you need some pampering."

From the bag, she pulled out various facial lotions that she had bought that afternoon just for me. "After treating your face each day, I want to follow up by giving you a 'spa' treatment on your healthy skin."

We all felt overwhelmed by such personal care and offered to pay for the products. But Jenny refused. "This is my treat."

As my sister and Mom gathered around and deferred the pain by grabbing my ankles, Jenny cleaned the area and re-bandaged me. The process was agonizing, but I knew it was necessary. She then placed new bandages over the entire left side of my face in preparation for the next day.

By the time she was done, most of the medical staff were long gone. In the quiet office, not only was my face being treated, but also my tender soul was being nourished. Mom,

Lauri, and I left that afternoon blown away by such expertise and compassion. On our way home, we thanked God for the amazing connection with such a gifted and caring nurse.

⌒

Because Jenny was coming to our home on Saturday, she called Friday evening to give me a list of things for Tom to buy at the pharmacy—a recommended ointment, latex gloves, and various bandaging materials. "I'll see you tomorrow at your home."

On Saturday morning, in preparation for Jenny's treatment, I brought in a white plastic recliner from the backyard and set it up in the family room. I covered it with a cushy blanket. On our coffee table, I placed all the medical treatment supplies Tom had just bought. Our family room looked like a mini triage center.

Jenny arrived, and we laughed at the idea of being treated on a lawn recliner. "Hey, it will keep my head from moving while you work on my face, just like at the office."

My family grabbed my ankles and wrists as usual, which did seem to help defer the pain. Jenny had a difficult time removing the bandaging and cleaning the left side of my face. She wanted to be very careful to leave the large area of newly growing skin intact. Thankfully, the screaming pain from the skin cleaning subsided as soon as she placed ointment onto the open wound. I kept my eyes shut. I have a weak stomach for such things.

I soon realized that I was the only queasy one in my family when it came to gruesome-looking wounds. Tom,

Lauri, and Mom all watched the entire procedure without wincing. When Jenny offered to show me my wounds once again with a mirror, I responded, "No way!"

I thought it was hilarious when Lauri excitedly began clicking away with her camera, taking multiple close-ups. "I just love this stuff."

Above all, I was so glad that Mom and Lauri could witness what seemed to be a very promising new start. Their presence helped me cope. Afterward, we all talked as Jenny once again gave me a spa treatment to help lighten my outlook. My agonizing wound care was followed by a balm of refreshment. What a treat.

We discovered that this delightful nurse had extensive nursing training and had done specialized wound care for nine years. I could not believe how fortunate I was to be connected with her. I thanked her profusely for being willing to care for and try to help heal me.

On Sunday, Jenny treated both the left and right sides of my face. The project was expanding quickly and becoming more complex. "Kristi, I'm learning that if I remove the bandaging all at once, one area dries out too much while I work on the other. So from now on I will work on only one portion at a time."

After finishing her work that afternoon, Jenny told me, "I've decided that I don't want anyone else to handle your case. It's too complicated." I felt blessed to know that my face would be in the hands of such a gifted expert. Finally, someone knew what to do and was doing it!

Chapter 27

A Healer

Jenny began tackling my forehead on Monday. It was the most deeply damaged area and also the largest. I needed to take additional Extra-Strength Tylenol. I would have loved to have taken something much stronger.

"I'm trying a variety of ointments and emollients to find the best moisture balance," Jenny said. "We don't want the wounds to get too wet or too dry." I appreciated that she was being innovative, learning along the way.

Our family all felt excited that the process was proving to be successful so far. As Mom felt a new surge of hope and relief for my burden, she began thinking of her own personal burden in a new light. "Now, maybe I will find a solution for my breast cancer, too!"

Mom and Lauri could now return home knowing that I was in good hands. They could rest. I could rest. There would be an end someday. We didn't know when, but it now seemed assured.

Most encouraging for me was knowing that my skin really could heal normally. I'd been to at least twelve skin-related doctors over the past six months, and some of these health experts had wondered why I had not yet healed. "Maybe you have an immunology issue." Now it was confirmed. My skin just needed to be given the right kind of wound care treatment, and then it could heal very well.

Jenny's work on my face was certainly complicated and time consuming. I soon detected tension at the clinic while I was being treated. I discovered that patients were typically allotted only twenty-minute appointments, while my facial treatments took close to two hours.

Early on, Jenny also shared with Tom and me that some of the medical staff did not think she should be treating my face at all. They told her that a face problem like mine should be left to a dermatologist. "Besides," they warned, "what if your patient sues you for being scarred?"

I immediately told her, "Jenny, you don't need to worry about me ever suing you. I was told long ago that I would be scarred. I just want to have skin back on my face."

After all, I knew that a person can't have crusting stuck in her face for close to six months without permanent damage. I admired Jenny for her willingness to take such a complicated case against so many obstacles.

So Jenny kept working on the different parts of my face as long as she thought she needed to. She painstakingly removed the different bandages, gently cleaned my wounds, and carefully rebandaged me, always adjusting to what she was discovering.

Tom made an observation as he watched her work. "Jenny is not just a health care provider. She is a healer. In other words, she cares about the whole person being restored and not just the body parts."

I went to the wound care clinic on Mondays, Wednesdays, and Fridays, and Jenny came to our home on the remaining days. A wide variety of friends picked me up and joined me as comrades in my wound care treatment program. At the clinic, I asked them to grab my ankles during the cleaning process to defer the pain. Sometimes the way one of my friends grabbed an ankle made me feel ticklish. It was so strange to want to laugh and cry simultaneously. One of my friends put her grand-mothering skills to work and sang, "The eensy weensy spider went up the waterspout." I couldn't help smiling while wincing in pain.

One afternoon, as I waited for Jenny to arrive, the medical assistant took my blood pressure.

"Umm … Kristi," she remarked, "Your blood pressure is so low that I am legally required to admit you to the hospital. Do you feel faint?"

"No," I responded. "How about if I jog in place for a bit to get my body going?"

"That should help."

I gladly jogged for about a minute, and she retook my blood pressure. "Yeah, it's good enough now." I assumed it was moving back toward my normal low range of 90/60.

As I had wondered earlier, I wondered once again. *Have my meds affected my blood pressure—making it plum-*

met? I felt physically cold most of the time. Sometimes at Tom's office, even while wearing a sweater, I'd go into another room that had a huge window that got direct sunlight. I pressed my hands against the glass trying to heat up my freezing body. If my antibiotics tended to lower my blood pressure, that might explain the physical reactions where I sometimes felt that my body wanted to quit, or my heart felt like it didn't want to beat.

Jenny arrived each day always positive and enthusiastic, and she regularly took pictures of my face to document its progress. It warmed my heart to experience her contagious excitement when she could see my skin healing over the wounded areas. She was genuinely thrilled with the progress, and she lit up the room.

During my skin treatments, I never outright cried in front of her, though I could feel tears filling my eyes when the pain became extreme. Nor did I complain when a treatment day presented a setback. Here was this incredible nurse willing to give her time and energy to help me. I did not want to show her how utterly distressed I felt each day from the pain for fear that she might quit. Jenny worked faithfully and creatively, always considering and trying various options. She was my one and only hope. There was virtually no one else I could imagine who would be willing to make such a sacrifice or who had the ability to do what she was trying to accomplish.

We did have setbacks. Sometimes the bandaging became too dry. Jenny would warn me, "This is going to be painful, Kristi, because the new skin got stuck to the bandage and will come off with it."

Sometimes when a bandage was left on too long, the skin became "macerated" (like when one's skin gets too wet while sitting in a bathtub). When brand-new skin becomes macerated, it becomes too damaged to leave in place. Jenny would apologize, "Sorry, but I'm going to have to remove your new skin in this area. It's not viable because it got too moist."

Eventually Tom could detect the subtle changes in my wounds from one session to another. He noticed my skin growing in unique directions, creating interesting shapes, until the wound had only little spots remaining, requiring less and less care.

Throughout the days of treatment, I prayed, "God, please help Jenny know what to do as she is trying various techniques. And, God, please help her to be brave and willing to treat me although others might try to discourage her. And please, please I beg of you, don't let her quit. I know she's so extremely busy with her other patients. And above all, thank you for Jenny, that I finally found someone who could help heal me."

Through trial and error, Jenny's effort took things in a definite forward-moving direction. Eventually, she determined which parts of my "infant" skin were strong enough to hold. She kept those areas open to the air. After eleven long days, I asked her, "How much of my face has fully healed?"

"Your left side is about 25 percent healed," she said. "Your right side is about 40 percent, and your forehead about 15 percent."

I'd been enduring so much pain for so long and was hoping my recovery would be further along. "I feel a bit discouraged," I told her.

Since she took pictures almost every day, Jenny scrolled through them on her camera and showed me some of the visible progress. "See, Kristi, look how much more skin is showing. And some of these areas no longer need a bandage."

Yes, I could see positive changes.

"So don't be concerned. Your skin is doing great. I'm very encouraged about your progress, and you should be too. You are going to heal."

I began to wonder whether Jenny was paid for the days that she treated my face at our home. Here she was, working sixty hours a week at various wound care facilities with many patients and adding my crazy case to her heavy load. She even took on the workload of a vacationing doctor for a week during my treatment time. I felt so guilty, but we did not have any other option.

As the bandaging became increasingly complicated, Jenny became all the more creative with her bandage cutting. My face became a kaleidoscope of interesting shapes. Always trying to keep things light, she named the bandages according to their unique configurations. One she named a duck, another a pair of bloomers, and another a fireplace mantel with a stocking. I don't know how she knew exactly how to cut the tiny, intricate shapes that became so important to my full recovery. And I couldn't imagine any other medical professional who would be willing to take the kind of time that she did to get it right.

Chapter 28

⌒

Wounding Wounds

Jenny was now working on my entire face every day. My forehead treatment was so extensive and painful I asked that she start with that wound area first. Once my forehead was done, I could relax much more as she proceeded.

Tuesdays were Jenny's busiest days, so she could not treat my face until late in the evening at our home. I was just glad that she came at all. Leaving the bandaging on my face that extra time could possibly cause parts of my skin to become too wet and macerated. Timing really is everything when it comes to specialized wound care.

One Tuesday night, Jenny apologized because she couldn't come until quite late. The bandages on my face had been left on an extra six hours. After she removed them she noted, "Your entire forehead is macerated. I don't have time to treat it tonight. Please take extra pain meds before you come in tomorrow. I will need to remove your entire forehead."

If I were one to cuss, I would have blurted some appropriate expletive. Instead I just said, "Oh, no. Yikes!"

⌒⌒

I braced myself for what was to come on Wednesday afternoon, popping Extra-Strength Tylenol early in the day and then doubling the dosage to try to build it up in my system. A dear friend, Barb, from our home group had volunteered to be my Wednesday designated driver. She came in dressed in her cute tennis outfit, picked me up at home, and drove me to the clinic. Together we froze in the air conditioning as we waited. Nurse Jenny finally arrived, and Barb grabbed my ankles hard. The dreaded removal of my bad skin commenced.

Jenny began on the right side of my forehead and moved across. She kept me posted along the way regarding the percentage that she had removed. First, 25 percent, then 50 percent, then 75 percent, and almost done. Yes, the worst was finally over.

Afterward I felt like a shattered shell of a person. As Barb and I walked into the elevator, just one other person joined us. I leaned on the hand railing to avoid collapsing. Barb guided me to the foyer area downstairs to wait while she went to get her SUV. Looking out the large window, I leaned against a wall. I felt utterly broken, weeping inside. *I just want to go home. I don't want to keep on doing this. It's just too hard.*

I cannot explain what it feels like to have one's entire forehead peeled off. I could feel blood seeping out of the bandaging.

When Barb drove up to the building in her car, I slowly walked out and gingerly got into the back seat. As I sat silently in physical shock, Barb finally spoke up, "I want to get you something to eat. I think you could use a boost."

"There's a juice bar on the way home." So we stopped and Barb bought me a favorite strawberry-flavored smoothie. As we drove, both of us knew being quiet was best. Arriving home, she helped walk me into the house. After she quietly left, I sat on our love seat and cried.

I talked with Tom that night. "This was such a horrifying day, but Jenny is still optimistic. She told me, 'Don't worry, your forehead will grow back.'"

When I saw Jenny the following day, she immediately told me, "There was a man on the elevator with you yesterday. He actually came back up to our office to ask me, 'Is that lady going to be okay?' He was really concerned, so I reassured him you were going to be fine, and you are moving forward."

Despite the horrendous day, Jenny and I continued onward. I did not cry or complain about the pain and distress that I felt as she painstakingly and carefully cleaned my wounds once again. I was just so grateful that she had found the solution for my wounded face and was determined to see me all the way through.

⟡

Although my face was still covered with many bandages and going through intensive wound care, Tom and I decided to visit Dr. Palik and Dr. Joy. We wanted to show them my great progress. We thought they'd be encouraged.

When Dr. Palik saw me, he was indeed excited. He asked for Jenny's number. "I want to personally thank her." Just before Tom and I left, he spoke to me. "Kristi, when I saw you for the first time months ago, I almost walked straight back out of the room. My office staff had indicated with rolled eyes that said, 'You won't believe what's behind that door,' and I was shocked to see the combination of the redness from the laser and the yellow fluid over that. Your face looked orange."

I laughed and thanked him for hiding his true feelings on that first day back in June. To me, he seemed like one of the calmest people I'd ever met.

Then he added, "I am very proud of you for keeping on looking for answers."

Those words meant a great deal to me. They felt monumental. I knew Dr. Palik had been frustrated with me at times for going down divergent paths over the past six months, especially after the fateful home misting treatment disaster. Now, I had finally found the answer and we could celebrate together.

Likewise, when Tom and I saw Dr. Joy, she was thrilled to see how well my face was healing. She asked me to bring in the beauty products that Jenny was using, "I want to check their safety for your delicate skin." I appreciated both doctors' continued involvement and care.

As my skin grew in, filling the wounded areas, the procedure was becoming less time consuming and far less painful. My face still looked scary, now becoming bright red where the new portions of skin were exposed. I was concerned that it looked so raw, but Jenny promised me that it was healthy skin and "holding," whatever that meant.

As friends and family began to hear the news, they all expressed excitement and gratefulness that Jenny had figured out a lasting solution for my face. Tom and I thanked her over and over. Despite being on a high learning curve and doing such tedious work, she was doing a phenomenal job. She never gave up.

About two weeks into the treatments, I saw myself in the bathroom mirror downstairs. And for the first time in a long time what looked back at me was the real me.

"There you are," I said to myself. "I'm coming back."

I could now feel breezes on my face—such a light and delightful feeling. Awesome.

✺

We were now on the home stretch, only seven spots of tiny bandages remained. One evening Jenny called. "I have absolutely no time to see you at the clinic or at your home tomorrow. My schedule is far too packed. Would you be able to meet me in the women's bathroom on the second floor of the building where the wound care clinic is? I think two o'clock will work. That way I can quickly treat your face between changes of location."

"Sure. No problem. I'll see you there."

The following afternoon, I packed all my wound-care paraphernalia and a beach towel. My ever-faithful

Wednesday driver, Barb, took me to the clinic, and we met Jenny at the rendezvous point.

The three of us laughed as we squished into the handicapped stall. After placing the medical supplies onto the beach towel that I placed on the floor, Jenny put on her rubber gloves. She tried to treat me while I stood up. Since I was taller than she was, that idea didn't work, so, I sat down on the toilet. Barb handed Jenny supplies. She quickly cleaned my skin and applied new bandages. I wondered what the other women coming and going must have thought to hear the three of us bantering inside the bathroom stall. The treatment time probably took less than ten minutes.

As we walked out, I now considered Jenny my special "nurse on the go," boldly going where no nurse normally would go.

Chapter 29

_◯_

A New Me

At three weeks and two days from the first day I met Jenny, she made a pronouncement as she finished treating my face at her office, "Kristi, you now have intact skin."

Momentous words.

For the first time in six months, my skin had grown back together and was connected as it should be. It was now mid-September.

Her sacrificial service and gifted expertise had achieved the seemingly impossible. Tom, Jenny, and I celebrated. "You might need just a few more treatments—just touch-ups."

I had a lot of questions. "Jenny, can I eat any kind of food now? I don't have to use a straw?"

"Yes, you can eat whatever you like."

"Can I take a shower?"

"Yes."

"Are you sure? Will my skin stay on? The last time I got into a shower, it didn't go so well."

"Yes, you can shower as much as you like."

I couldn't believe it.

⟨⟨

It was a Friday. Jenny asked me, "Kristi, when was the last time you had anything done with your hair?"

"I've been wearing it in a ponytail since March 8th."

She joked, "I'm tired of looking at your hair pulled back into a ponytail. I'm done with work early today, so I think I'll see if I can get you in to my salon." An hour later she called, saying, "I have an appointment. Give me directions to Tom's office. I'll pick you up there."

Jenny pulled up in her sporty black car and whisked me off to a nice little salon. I was afraid I might frighten the other people there since my face was still markedly red and raw-looking, but I think Jenny had forewarned them. There were just a couple other clients getting their hair done in booths far away.

After the stylists washed and highlighted my hair, I was horrified to see how thin it had become. I figured my hair loss had something to do with the months of stress or perhaps from taking so many meds.

In the end I loved the outcome. The stylist gave me a cute shorter cut, with slightly tapered bangs. I smiled from ear to ear, feeling like a lady once more.

When Jenny dropped me off at the back of our house, I wanted her to meet my neighbor, Julie. So many months ago Julie had driven me to see Dr. Joy when I knew something was terribly wrong. Now, six months from that infamous day in March, I had skin back on my face and a new 'do to match. Julie came by and was deeply impressed by all that Jenny had accomplished and thrilled to see my full recovery. She took a picture of Jenny and me in the back driveway. Hugging one another, we celebrated.

It was wonderful to eat regular food again. No straws were needed anymore! And I could laugh and cry, and even sneeze without pain. And I could now brush my teeth easily once again. Life was certainly turning back to normal.

The first time I stepped into the shower, I felt petrified. *Jenny said I could do this. She said my face skin would hold this time. Okay, here goes.* I turned on the water and cautiously put my face under the shower head, and then quickly touched my cheeks and forehead. *So far, so good. Yes, my skin is staying on!* Then I turned and placed both of my hands on the tile wall, as the water blasted away, and began bawling like I had never done before. "Oh, God, Oh, God, this has been such a horrible nightmare!" I wailed and wailed and wailed. For the past six months I had wanted to cry so hard, but I had to be so controlled. At last I could fully express the terror I had felt, the heart-ache of doors closing one after another, the months of pain and looking so distorted, and despite being with people trying to help, feeling so desperate and alone. I cried out to God repeatedly. "Oh, God, this has been so hard! God, this has been so hard!" I turned back as I sobbed, and for a long while I let the shower water pour down my face, washing away my salty tears.

❧

My face wasn't out of the woods quite yet. In late September, Tom was taking his biannual trip to the warehouse in Pennsylvania where goods for humanitarian aid were packed and shipped for distribution overseas. Jenny gave me the okay to go with him. Since Tom's parents lived nearby, it would be a treat to see them and show them my newly healed face.

The night before we left, Jenny called. "I left a surprise package for you on your front porch." Opening the door, I saw a lovely multi-colored orange, brown, and beige bag. Inside were magazines and fun books for me to read on the trip. Attached was a note wishing me the best on being able to travel again. Another incredibly thoughtful gift from the amazing person who had already given me so much.

I am sure I looked really strange to all who saw me at the airport. After all, who hasn't seen a woman with an ultra-sunburned red face with a white neck and arms? I imagined that I wasn't so noticeable because Tom was with me, and he looked normal.

❧

After we enjoyed a few delightful days with Tom's parents, we drove out to the distribution center. I sat in the back seat covering my face with a brochure with two eye holes cut out of it. I didn't want to miss the lovely hilly countryside, gorgeous stone houses, and the farmlands of Lancaster County, PA. I was delighted to see an Amish farmer cultivating a field with a team of horses. Two children in colorful frocks pulled a red wagon in which a white duck sat contentedly. What a beautiful drive.

Once we reached the warehouse, Tom and I got caught up with both staff and volunteer friends. Many had prayed for me over the previous six months. Some said, "What matters is the inward person and not the outward appearance." Although absolutely true, that phrase didn't always encourage me, as I still looked like a roasted tomato.

Later that afternoon, one of Tom's friends, Brian, came up and told us his own burn story. Scars covered the right side of his face, neck and arm. "Several years ago I was severely burned when pouring an accelerant on a campfire. The explosion hit my right side. I jumped into the lake, and watched my burnt skin hanging down in the water." He then admitted, "I actually begged the hospital staff to kill me when I had to sit in the whirlpool to slough off the dead tissue. The pain was so excruciating." I realized that this man had suffered far beyond what I could ever imagine, and yet here he was, scars covering a side of his face and arm, joyfully investing his life for others through organizing humanitarian aid. Together we talked about God's grace and agreed that having "skin on" was a tremendous blessing that we no longer took for granted.

The longer I was away in Pennsylvania, the more I realized I still needed some expert wound care. I studied my face and saw a few of the healing spots had become increasingly oozy. Even some of our friends expressed their concerns. "Kristi, your skin is looking a lot worse now than it was a week ago when you first got here."

"Yeah, I know, but I'm going to wait until I get back to Texas. My nurse will be able to fix it there. I don't want to mess with it." For the rest of the week, I tried not to worry but enjoy our time in beautiful Pennsylvania with Tom's parents.

Upon returning home, Jenny graciously came over to our house and did some much-needed tweaking. She occasionally stopped by over the next six weeks to touch up a few of the temperamental spots, until I was fully, fully healed. I still never knew whether she was ever paid for treating my face at our home.

⌒

One day when she came over I said, "Jenny, I think I want to go back to church with Tom on Saturday night. What do you think? Is it an option?"

"Yes," she said as she studied my face, "but I'd like to help you with your makeup. It could be complicated." Jenny came by the house on Saturday afternoon and brought with her a colorful bag full of lipstick, mascara, a powder foundation, and brushes—all just for me.

As she tried to apply the foundation, I could tell that even for Jenny it was an arduous task. She was somewhat successful and my face was covered, but it still was weird looking. The foundation got stuck in the undulations of my skin, but it did mask much of the redness.

That evening I realized as soon as Tom and I sat down in church that I must still look unusual. People were turning around to look at me. They weren't trying to be rude, but obviously my face still stood out. It was kind of embarrassing, so as soon as the service was over I scooted out the side doors and back out to the car. I thought I would wait a while longer before venturing out again.

ᴄᴏ

It just so happened the next day, my friend Kelli (the friend who first drove me to see Dr. Palik so many months earlier) called me. "I want to take you to one of the makeup counters at Dillard's. I know they carry a foundation specifically designed to cover scars and other undesirable marks. Do you have time to go with me today?"

"Sure. That idea sounds like it could be a good option."

When we arrived at the mall, I felt conspicuous walking with Kelli through the high-end department store to the counter where the special makeup was sold. Two consultants approached us.

When we explained my facial issues and a bit of my story, they said that they would give the concealing makeup a try.

Cautiously they began. "Let's just put this on the lower left part of your face to see how it will work."

The makeup provided wonderful coverage! We all unanimously agreed. "Let's do half of Kristi's face."

We laughed as now one-half of my face was transformed to "normal" while the other half remained bright red.

"I think we should go for it. Let's do my whole face."

Once done, we celebrated. Perfect success! My red face now had a normal looking skin tone. Amazing! I couldn't believe it. After buying the concealer, I asked Kelli, "Would it be okay if I looked around the department nearby for a little while?"

"Sure. Take your time."

I hadn't shopped in seven months, so this was exciting. I ventured to the close by lingerie section and found some long-sleeved undershirts for Mom. They would help her stay cozy in rainy Seattle. To my great surprise, the young woman who checked me out treated me as if I were a normal person, just like everyone else. I was blending into life again, and it felt wonderful!

⌒

Now that Jenny had finished treating my face, Tom and I wanted to give her a special gift. But what could we possibly give this nurse that would even come close to adequately thanking her for saving my life on so many levels? We had one idea. I had done several paintings that hung on the walls of our home. And I had previously shown them to Jenny.

I called her up. "Is there one of my paintings in our home that you would like to have? If so, I would like to make a print of it for you." She picked out a favorite.

The watercolor she selected was a scene of a New England church. Its steeple is silhouetted against a yellowish evening sky. Purple-hued storm clouds seem to be floating away as the storm dissipates. A few birds fly freely in the early evening calm. I had named this piece, "Evening Respite." Although I painted it three years before, in many ways it reflected the recent long ordeal I had been through and now was on the other side of.

I found a printmaker who made a beautiful copy from my original. When Tom and I presented the framed print to Jenny, we shared from our hearts. "Jenny, we want to express to you our profound gratefulness for all the time, loss of your sleep, tedious and hard work, and your incredible guts and stamina day after day. Above all, you showed such genuine compassion. We cannot thank you enough, but this is a small token of our appreciation."

Others who had heard about her dedicated efforts wanted to thank Jenny tangibly as well. One friend gave her a gas gift card. Other women from our home group gave her a variety of gift cards as I told them that she loved The Body Shop, MacDonald's coffee, and certain local restaurants. I created a bouquet of gift cards for her, and together some of my friends presented them to Jenny.

Jenny and I kept in touch and even enjoyed a double date with our husbands. From time to time, we enjoyed catching up over a robust breakfast at a lovely local restaurant. I can only imagine that she continues to make this world a better place as she uses her life so effectively, giving life and hope to countless patients and their families.

I wanted Jenny to be publicly acknowledged on a grand scale. She never was. But now you know about this remarkable woman. She should be heralded as a person who represents the best of the best in the medical field. She is an expert nurse with a relentless passion to see that the most difficult cases are given the best outcomes, often at great personal sacrifice. She went beyond the normal call of duty. She brought full healing to me, both physically and emotionally.

Jenny became the answer when I had no hope. I have thanked God regularly for her. "Lord, bless Jenny, wherever she may be."

Chapter 30

࿎

Plastic Face

Although my face had skin on it, it had been "through a war" and still had a long way to go to fully heal. A few weeks after I "got my skin on," it was time to see the burn doctor, Dr. Drake. I met with him and another burn specialist recommended by Dr. Joy. As both experts studied my face, they were pleased with what they saw.

Dr. Drake said, "This week I'd like you to come back to be fitted with a plastic mask. The compression of the mask will help your face heal more evenly and prevent further scarring. You'll need to wear it at all times except when eating."

"Can I skip wearing it when out in public?"

Both doctors simultaneously said, "No. No one will notice it anyway."

I almost burst out laughing. *You've got to be kidding me. Wearing a shiny clear plastic mask showing bright red skin will certainly be noticeable in public.*

The next day Tom and I returned to the burn clinic for the fitting process. Unfortunately, the night before Tom accidentally jammed his foot, spraining his big toe. Together we looked like quite the pair as we came into the office. Tom gingerly hobbled in while I, the red-faced woman, walked by his side.

We were taken into a large room where we could see other patients being treated for burns. One nurse unwrapped a man's left hand as his wife looked on. He had only stubs for fingers. The discouragement on his face was profound.

As soon as my nurse came in, she instructed me to sit down on an examination table. "Remain seated, for this is the best position for the plaster-cast procedures. When a person lies down, the facial shape changes. Don't move your face as I plaster it."

First, she covered my face with a greasy ointment. Then she mixed up some white plaster and proceeded to apply it to my entire face, avoiding my eyes, nostrils, and mouth. I sat still for about fifteen minutes until the plaster fully hardened. She returned, and with some effort pulled off the mask in one piece. "Come back tomorrow. I will need to prepare your mask."

As we concluded our session, a boy about ten years old was wheeled in. Half of his face looked like that of a very scarred old man. The other half looked normal. Both of his arms were blackened from his fingertips to his shoulders.

I could only imagine that before the burns this boy had been running around, carefree, hanging out with his friends and family, living life as a child should. Now, he would have to endure unimaginable pain, and his entire future had been changed. No more carefree days. How would other children react to him from now on? Undoubtedly, his face and arms would be severely scarred. The staff carefully moved the boy to a large platform. His face reflected his agony. I couldn't bear to watch. I turned away and walked out with the nurse into the hallway.

"What might have happened to cause that boy such burns?"

She said, "For many children burns are due to playing with fire, gasoline, or fireworks. If their clothes or hair catch on fire, they are in deep trouble."

After seeing this young boy in such horrifying agony, my situation seemed relatively mild. I had it so easy compared to what burn victims have had to endure. The misery of that place gave me perspective.

⌒

Tom and I returned the following afternoon to the burn hospital and were escorted to an unusual room. Cement heads were lined up on a high shelf. It was strange to see in the middle of the room a cement cast of my head mounted on a steel pole. I found out that the clinicians first make the cement cast from the plaster mold and then form a plastic mask from that cast. The nurse placed my mask onto the cement head, and then using a small electric cutting tool, she drilled holes for my eyes, nose, and mouth.

Several times she placed the mask against my face and removed it to make adjustments. "I want to ensure that your skin will not be irritated since you will be wearing this most of each day. Please let me know if you feel any rough edges." After a few more touch-ups, the mask felt reasonably comfortable. "I need to put on some Velcro straps and then you can go."

She taught me how to strap on the mask. Feeling self-conscious, I wore it out of the office. It would become a major part of my life.

⌀

"Mask wearing" did take some adjusting. I quickly learned that I could not sleep in the mask, since moving from side to side caused it to dig into my skin. Hollowed indentations developed around my eyes as the mask pulled in against my face. And if it moved to one side or the other too much, the skin under that area would bruise. Despite all the hassles, keeping my skin flattened as it recovered was a blessing.

I rarely wore the mask in public, although I knew that I was violating doctors' orders. I didn't wear it to church, but I always wore it to our home group. After all, my friends there were used to seeing me looking strange. When I ran an occasional errand, I took it off briefly while in the store and put it back on as soon as I got back to the car. What a treat to be able to even run an occasional errand. Tom tried to encourage me as I wore my plastic face. "You actually look like one of those NBA players who wear masks in games to protect their faces after injuries."

The mask did not make me feel like an NBA player at all.

By early November, my skin was doing well. I attributed it to wearing the mask the majority of every day. At this time, Tom and I wanted to gather together the three primary medical staff who had walked me through my facial saga. We wanted to thank Dr. Joy for seeing me initially and staying with me for so long. We also wanted to thank Dr. Palik for hanging in there with me for all the twists and turns of my healing process, and we wanted to thank Jenny for being instrumental in getting me fully healed. Each had played a significant role in my recovery. We also wanted to give these medical experts an opportunity to meet one another. Perhaps in the future they could share their expertise.

Remarkably, we found a lunchtime when Dr. Joy (dermatologist extraordinaire), Dr. Palik (infectious disease expert), and Jenny (superstar RN) had free time and could all come together. I did not wear my plastic mask that day! Tom and I met them at a lovely restaurant downtown, fitted out with starched white-clothed tables and fine china. As we treated them to a delectable lunch, we caught up, sharing bits of our lives.

During lunch Dr. Joy said to me, "Kristi, I want you to come by the office so we can treat the extreme redness in your face. It's not going to go away on its own."

I had thought it would eventually go away. Apparently I was wrong. I appreciated her willingness to continue to help. I sure didn't want my face to look like I had a major sunburn the rest of my life.

At the conclusion of our meal, I gave each of them a folder with pictures of my face illustrating its progress along the way. I also included a brief writeup of what had transpired through the many months. I placed some humorous quotes at the end, such as Dr. Joy telling me, "If you want me to use maggots, I'm off your case!"

Tom and I hugged each of them good-bye, and expressed our joy in their sacrifice and faithful service on my behalf. I wished I had taken a picture of the mighty trio, but they are forever in my mind and heart.

~

The next week I met with Dr. Joy at her office. She explained her concern. "As long as there is deep redness, your face will tend to scar, even if you wear the compression mask. I want you to heal with as little scarring as possible." She went on to explain her recommendation. "There is a pulsed dye laser that works well in removing wine stain birthmarks, the dark red-purple coloration, from the skin. The laser bruises the skin and as the capillaries naturally drain away the bruising, the redness goes away with it. This process should work for you."

She gave me a cost estimate for several treatments. They would be expensive, so on her own initiative she suggested, "I'm sending a letter to Dr. Anders requesting that he pay for this part of your recovery. I feel that if a patient gets damaged through a treatment in an office, the doctor in charge should pay for it."

For a trial run, Dr. Joy applied the laser to one square inch of my forehead. When I came back a week later for her inspection, she noted, "This is working great!" So she treated my entire face. "By the way, I never heard back from Dr. Anders." Just as I expected. He would not help.

Even with pre-applied numbing cream, a pulsed dye laser feels like someone is taking a rubber band and flicking the skin over and over. I felt like my face was hit with multiple bee stings. After a day or so, the laser had produced what looked like dozens of purple dots about a quarter of an inch apart that covered my entire face. It took ten days for the spots to go away, and as predicted my facial redness diminished. So the procedure proved very promising. We would continue after the Christmas break with further treatments.

Chapter 31

JO

Christmas

Tom and I were thrilled. Not only was my face healing nicely, but we were going to visit my parents' home in Seattle for Christmas. Close to five months had passed since Mom's last visit and it had been almost a year since I saw my dad. Family members were coming in from all over the country for the holiday, from California, Texas, and Florida. Daughters, sons-in-law, an aunt and uncle, nieces and nephews, along with many grandchildren all flew in for this festive occasion.

But for me there was a sadness to the festivities. Mom's cancer was progressing rapidly. She had tried many alternative treatments and a few standard cancer procedures. Watching her, I had a sense that she did not feel well physically at all, but I knew she had gone all out to have her home nicely decorated and to provide tasty foods for our arrival. She loved hosting family.

Dad had had Parkinson's disease for more than nine years and was living in a group home that offered round-the-clock nursing and care. I couldn't wait to see him. On the first evening we all piled into cars and headed over to where he was so lovingly cared for. The staff at his home, who felt more like family, had cheerfully decorated the family and dining rooms for Christmas. A fire was lit in the fireplace as Christmas music played softly in the background. When I walked into Dad's bedroom, he looked up from his recliner with surprise. I hugged and kissed him.

He then looked concerned. "We have to do something about your face."

My sweet dad rarely said anything anymore, so I knew he was truly concerned about how red my face looked. As we talked further, he interrupted our conversation once again. "We have to do something to help your beautiful face."

Gently I told him, "I am getting help. It is actually much better than it used to be."

When Dad commented a third time about his concerns with my face, I took his concern as a sign of his deep compassion and love. As we wheeled him out to the family room, all of us bantered together and enjoyed being in his company. Once again I was reminded of how blessed I was to have such a wonderful, caring, beloved father.

⌒

At home, Mom was stoic. I could tell she was exhausted but with attentive care she hosted us with the most. She loved having family gathered all around. I appreciated how she had planned and paid for all of us to stay in a condo on Cannon Beach on the Oregon coast as part of our big family reunion. When she explained that she had driven herself out to the coast a few weeks prior to our arrival to confirm that it was just what she wanted, I felt upset that she drove so far on her own. A five-hour drive there and back. Such an act of heroic, loyal love.

During the first night at the cozy condo with a view of the ocean, our family played a favorite game—Cranium. I looked over to the kitchen where Mom watched us as we all laughed hysterically as we competed on teams. We had to hum tunes, draw pictures, spell complicated words backward, act out various characters, answer trivia questions, and make objects out of clay. Mom seemed to relax as she watched us enjoying ourselves. I was glad she could savor the joy of seeing many of her family gathered together. But at times she seemed lost in her own world.

The next day our family walked out to the beach in freezing cold weather. Mom did not have the strength to walk on the beach, so she went into town to visit favorite local shops. I tagged along and spent time with her looking at art galleries. Cannon Beach had been one of Dad and Mom's favorite vacation spots.

While there Mom noticed that *The Sound of Music* was being performed that evening by some local actors. We all decided to go, Mom's treat. It wasn't Broadway by any means, but it was still fun. As I sat in the same row with Mom and my sister Kari, I watched my dear mom looking out at the play with an expression of deep sadness and distraction. *Was she missing my dad? After all, throughout their life together they had loved traveling, going to plays, looking at art galleries and museums, and most of all, being with family. But Dad was not there. Surely she felt sad, perhaps reflecting that this might be the last Christmas she would have with all of us.* I shared her sadness.

We returned to Mom's home in Seattle to finish our holiday together. We managed to bring Dad to Mom's townhouse to join us. How delightful it was to watch everyone chatting, watching football games on TV, and eating delicious food.

Mom and Dad loved movies, so on our last night Mom wanted us to watch a recent release, *Amazing Grace.* Squeezing into the family room, we were transported to the passionate and strategic political world of William Wilberforce and his friends as they helped end the slave trade in England. We were reminded that a person who has a heart for the things of God has a heart to make an absolute difference in the lives of people, and not just talk about it.

Leaving Mom and Dad wasn't easy, but we returned home with fond and poignant memories.

❧

A few weeks later, we all received a large photo from Mom taken during our time in the Northwest. As soon as I saw the photo I burst out laughing. While visiting the Oregon coast our family had eaten ice cream together at the Tillamook Cheese Factory—a family favorite. Afterward, we took a group picture. Fifteen of us looked normal, and there I was on the front row smiling with a face that looked like it had been torched.

As I looked at my bright red face, I immediately thought of the Sesame Street song that goes, "Which of these things is not like the other?" Yup. My "queen of sunburns" face was a shocking standout.

Chapter 32

ɪᴏ

California, Here I Come

During the last day of our family Christmas gathering, my older sister, Kari, had mentioned she had an appointment scheduled with her renowned dermatologist in southern California on January 4th.

"Why don't you come and take my place?" she suggested. "Dr. Simpson already has your records and photos."

I immediately agreed, telling her, "Yes. I'll do it." I booked a flight to John Wayne airport for January 3rd.

I was excited to go to Los Angeles to visit Kari and get some fresh help. However, this would be the first time I traveled alone on a plane with my red face only partially concealed by makeup. I preferred not to wear the thick concealing makeup for it felt heavy on my skin and was hard to remove. Understandably, a woman sitting up one row across the aisle kept staring back at me throughout the flight. I thought she would get tired of looking, but she never did. My red face must have been fascinating to her. Turns out that would be the least disconcerting aspect of my late night flight.

Somewhere over the California desert the pilot announced, "Our flaps are not working, and we will need to use them when we land in about forty-five minutes." After pausing a moment he added, "As a precautionary measure our plane will be diverted to LAX, because LAX has really long runways." Not comforting.

Even more disconcerting was watching stewards and stewardesses walk up and down the main aisle studying a thick manual together. They rehearsed with us the importance of placing our heads between our legs before we landed. Over the intercom, the pilot said we would be coming in very "hot" and needed to be prepared.

I had a window seat. Just before we landed, the pilot commanded in loud, staccato tones, "Heads down now! Get your heads down now! Get your heads down now!" I took a quick glance out the window and saw that indeed we were coming in fast. *Yikes!*

We all braced ourselves for a hard landing. Yet we touched down with the softest landing I think I have ever had on any flight. We all clapped and cheered!

I looked out the window. Emergency vehicles were posted all along the runway with their flashing lights spinning. *Thank God we didn't need them.*

When it came time to deplane, I knew I had to stand up and become a spectacle. People who got glimpses of me seemed visibly surprised. I deduced that my face, having been between my knees for so long during our landing, must now look brighter than ever. I turned away from the other passengers as best I could and made a beeline for the airport ladies room. Looking in the bathroom mirror, I could see I was quite a sight. My face definitely needed some additional coverage.

Given the option to either take a short flight back to the John Wayne Airport in Orange County or travel by bus, we all enthusiastically opted for the bus. It was a long ride, and I was glad to see my sister in her dark navy Mustang at the other end.

❧

Early the next morning, I went with Kari to her dermatologist appointment. As she signed in, I grabbed a chair in the ultra-spa-like waiting room. A woman looking up at me from her magazine seemed visibly concerned. She asked politely, "What happened to your face?" Before I could answer she blurted out, "Did it happen at this office?"

My sister and I quickly reassured her. "Oh, no, her face problem didn't happen here."

"Dr. Simpson is quite good," Kari added. "We are actually here to get his help." The patient looked relieved and expressed her sympathies for my condition.

After a few minutes I said to Kari, "I think you need to let the receptionist know I am taking your place today. I can't just walk in." So together we approached Marge, the receptionist.

"No, your sister cannot take your appointment because first-time appointments take so much longer."

Kari tried to explain the serious nature of my facial condition and the need to see Dr. Simpson. Marge would not relent.

As we were trying to convince her of our case, one of the physician's assistants came up to the desk to turn in a medical file. As he stopped to talk with Kari, she introduced me and mentioned our dilemma.

As soon as he saw me, he seemed to recognize me. "I've seen your photos." I didn't know I was so famous. (I assumed he saw my photos when I sent them months ago to Dr. Simpson.) He spoke to Marge. "Dr. Simpson would definitely want to see Kristi today." I was in!

⟡

Shortly after, we were escorted to an inner office. Dr. Simpson arrived. He was a kind looking man wearing a white lab coat. He explained his medical observations to his assistant as she took notes. He described my face with words like *profuse scarring*. It was jarring to hear my facial damage explained in such direct medical terms.

When the initial evaluation was completed, Dr. Simpson explained, "It is quite clear that too many layers of your skin were removed during the initial laser procedure. This gave you little chance to heal, and a great opportunity for infection and scarring."

I asked Dr. Simpson, "What are the yellowish areas under some parts of my face, right under the skin?"

"We should not see these," he said. "Because too much of your skin was removed, the underlying fat pockets are now showing through, just below the epidermal layer."

He explained to me that a laser procedure works by taking thin slices off the skin, layer by layer—sort of like slicing a loaf of bread. He noted that Dr. Anders, the physician who did my initial procedure, had been way too aggressive. "With a person of your skin type, I would take only one or two passes. We can always go back and do more later. Yet according to the records, your doctor took three and four passes." I remembered Anders proudly telling Tom and me after my procedure, "I tried to be very aggressive."

Aha! Now it all made sense. For the first time in ten months I had a clear answer regarding my facial nightmare. No wonder my skin did not heal normally. There wasn't enough skin left to heal easily because too many layers had been removed.

Dr. Simpson further explained that during a laser procedure, a doctor looks at the skin closely to see how many passes to take.

His nurse piped up, "And if one ever sees a yellowish color, they would immediately know that they went way too deep." Even his nurse knew that much.

Yet, when my face first was infected and would not heal back in March, Dr. Anders kept insinuating that something was wrong with my face's ability to heal. Yet he was the doctor who damaged my face by taking too many passes. So, his mishandling of my face and the subsequent infection had resulted in the many months of personal misery, loss, and fear. I was relieved to hear confirmation of what I had so long suspected that it was not my fault.

Dr. Simpson offered several positive options to help my scarred and damaged skin to heal better. "I first suggest we used specialized light therapy treatments called Omnilux, which stimulates the collagen in the skin for more lively function. I want you to use three moisturizing serums to keep your face in a healing mode. And I want to continue to use the same laser that Dr. Joy has used to minimize your skin's redness."

I liked that he was using a multi-pronged approach.

"Can you stay in the area for several months?" he asked.

"No, but I can stay for three weeks. Maybe I could come back later."

I began the Omnilux light treatments the following day. In the procedure room, I was given light-blocking goggles. While I lay on an exam table, a specialized device was placed close to my face. As soon as the room lights were turned off, the intense light blasted my face. Even while wearing the goggles I could see a bright orange-red color, sort of like looking at the sun through smoked lenses.

Even after several sessions, I did not get used to the process. But I used the time to pray, especially for Mom as she battled cancer. I also prayed for Dad and Tom and our family. I was always glad when the intense light shut off and I could just rest in the dark, waiting for a medical assistant to come back in. I did the light treatments three times each week, and within a number of days I could tell that my skin was actually healing better. I was in the hands of a professional I could trust.

Chapter 33

⟨✦⟩

Mom and I, and TV Time

During my time in California I was never bored or lonely. My niece and her baby of about nine months came by Kari's house, keeping us all entertained. Then about a week into my stay, my other sister, Lauri, called from Seattle.

"I'm bringing Mom to stay with you. She found a naturopath in southern California and is hopeful that he can help her fight her cancer."

Kari and I picked up Mom and Lauri at the airport two days later. I was shocked to see Mom emerge from the exit looking weak and thin. Lauri supported her weight and helped her into the car.

I was assigned to be Mom's designated driver each day, to take her to and from the medical center thirty minutes away. I had to come up quickly with a plan to protect my face from the sun when driving such a distance. My niece and I went off to Target to find something workable.

I picked up a large pair of sunglasses and some T-shirt material in a watery green-blue color to cover my lower face. The final touch was a blue stretchy headband about two and a half inches wide to protect my forehead from the intense California sun. When I got home, I cut the T-shirt apart and created a cotton covering that hooked onto the sunglasses. This would protect my lower face. Yeah, It looked as stylish as it sounds.

Each morning I took Mom to her appointment for intravenous treatments. The medical staff were trying to boost her energy level. Afterward, I dropped her off at Kari's house and headed to Dr. Simpson's office.

⌒

Mom and I had always loved watching movies together. So to keep ourselves from getting bored out of our gourds in the afternoon, we rented DVDs for entertainment. Mom propped her legs up lengthwise on the love seat to face the TV, while I sat on the sofa.

We watched a wide variety of movies. Some were great. Others were not so great. The most irritating one, which seemed as long as its title, *The Assassination of Jesse James by the Coward Robert Ford*, starred Brad Pitt and Casey Affleck. The movie included scenes of rival gangs killing one another, riding horses, killing more people, and riding horses some more. Despite being beautifully shot and having outstanding actors—the movie did have sixty-eight nominations with twenty-five wins—for some reason we couldn't wait for the movie to end. "Whew, at last that one is over."

Mom and I became very close during those days. Each afternoon it was hard to watch her expression of distress as she checked her watch, waiting until the designated time to take her pain meds. She had been on a heavy-duty pain-killer for a long time, but I now doubted it was giving her the relief she needed. Her last lab reports did not look good. Her cancer was spreading to her lungs and liver. The medical notes read: "Too many spots on her lungs to count."

On the positive side, I cooked yummy meals for Mom to help boost her body. We ate mashed potatoes, meatloaf, green beans—lots of comfort foods. I was encouraged to see her eating well again and regaining both weight and strength during the two weeks we spent together.

Meanwhile, my treatments were going well at Dr. Simpson's clinic. One day while I was walking down the hallway, a physician's assistant named Richard saw me, stopped, flipped on some fancy glasses, and peered at my forehead. "Just what I thought," he said, and off he walked.

Later that week Richard was assigned to treat me with the laser. I asked him, "What were you looking for in particular when you stopped and studied my face?"

"Oh," he said, "I wanted to see your skin up close to confirm what I thought."

"What did you see?"

"Your face is a textbook case for 'delayed wound healing syndrome.'"

"Really? Are you sure? What is that?"

"Wait here. I'll show you a picture." He left the room and brought back an enormous dermatology book. He opened it up to a picture of a woman's forehead, which looked just like mine.

"What's it called again?"

"Delayed wound healing syndrome. Delayed wound healing can occur when too many layers of skin are removed during a laser procedure." He clarified. "I read your records. Your original procedure was too invasive."

Now I had another key to the puzzle of my slow-healing face. My wounded face couldn't heal readily because of how it had been treated originally. I now also had a name for my damaged face malady.

Meanwhile, the Omnilux treatments were so effective that Dr. Simpson asked permission to use my photos at an upcoming dermatological conference.

"I want to show your face photos at the symposium to demonstrate how improper laser procedure practices can damage a face. I also hope the photos of your staph-infected face will help demonstrate the issues that can occur. Is that okay?"

"Sure. I am glad if I can be a help to anyone."

While in California, Mom regularly checked her e-mails. One day while I was sitting on a single mattress on the floor that I used at my sister's home, I heard a hymn coming from her computer. Mom was playing a song a friend had just sent her to encourage her as she dealt with her cancer, "Tis So Sweet to Trust in Jesus." As the beautiful music filled the room, my tears began to flow. Mom joined me on the mattress. Putting her arm around my shoulder, we sat together as I cried.

"This is just still so hard," She didn't say anything, but I knew she understood.

One of the joys of my time in California was hearing Mom chat every evening on the phone with family, especially with her brother and sister-in-law. She would come alive, bantering and laughing, perhaps forgetting her mission in California and her uncertain future.

⟨⟩

One day as we arrived back at Kari's house Mom said, "You know, as you drive me around, you look like a terrorist."

She was right. With my "face covering" connected to my dark glasses and a blue headband, I did indeed look like a terrorist. So we joked that as we drove my sister's Mustang on the California freeways, we looked like "the terrorist and the grandma." What a pair. I was surprised that I never got pulled over by cops. Thank goodness my sister's car had dark window tinting.

On a bright, sunny morning two weeks after Mom first arrived, I dropped her off at the airport. I made sure to take off my facial protection as we got close. I did not want to scare the airport security staff who directed the curb traffic.

As Mom departed, I felt encouraged to see that she was able to walk normally on her own. I thought about how our time together had been such a remarkable gift—-

-to be with her during these difficult places in both of our lives. I thanked God especially for her sake that we had been able to laugh and enjoy movies and have great times together and be with my sister and her family. I was grateful that I could serve her as she had so faithfully done for me through the years. Mom's condition and outlook had greatly improved. Mine as well. She had arrived broken and weakened and now seemed strengthened and hopeful. It was a time of emotional and physical healing for both of us.

Chapter 34

◡◯

Film Crew—Fun Diversion

Before my final week in California, our son Jonathan, called with an invitation. I had been able to see him and his wife, Liesal, at their Burbank home while having my face worked on. "Mom, I'm shooting a short independent film for a competition. It'll be a comedy with a Western theme. We're filming up in the hills north of LA. Do you want to come?"

"I'd love to." *This will be so fun!*

Early Friday morning, I drove out to the shoot location and pulled into the entrance on the private property. Suddenly, I was surrounded by the gorgeous, red-rocky California landscape. *Wow. What a perfect place for a Western film shoot.*

When I parked with the other cars, I could see Jon and the crew setting up for the day. Because I didn't plan to wear my mask, I needed to be especially careful in the sun. It took a while to put on two layers of SPF 75 sunscreen and then apply my coverup makeup over that. Wearing a wide-brimmed hat and still feeling a bit vulnerable, I got out of the car.

It was fun meeting the twenty or so people at the shoot, and I was entertained seeing the actors in their authentic, Western-looking costumes. Working in cohesive fashion, each person, whether in sound, lighting, or film, did his or her job with expertise. Jon had a great crew and actors to work with. I tried to find shade wherever I could, leaning near the huge rocks or under scruffy bushes.

Unfortunately, airplanes from the Burbank's Bob Hope Airport seemed to take their flight paths right through the middle of some of the scenes. Someone would call "action," and then we would hear the drone of a plane in the distance and need to "cut" the scene until the plane passed by. Jon and his film team laughed as they looked at the "dailies" after the shoots. In one of the crucial scenes, a Southwest Airlines plane was clearly visible flying between the two bounty hunters. They would later remedy the plane problem by "clouding it out" on the computer in the final cut.

The second day of shooting was so incredibly windy and cold that I sat in one of the vehicles for most of the day. Fortunately, Jon was shooting the escape scenes as the bounty hunters chased the runaway bandits. There was little dialogue needed. I was grateful that my face was safe from the sun.

In preparation for the lunch break, one of the co-producers and I tried to set up the paper plates despite the wind. But we gave up as the plates became airborne, flying off in all directions. Some of the crew sat bravely outside at the wooden picnic tables, contending with the crazy wind, while holding down their plates and cups with great agility.

The rest of us crammed inside a van for a brief reprieve from the fierce winds. What a relief for me not to have to keep holding onto my wide-brimmed hat with an iron grip. As I watched from the side door, I admired the focus of everyone. For the film crew, the wind was merely a distraction, requiring adjustments.

The last day of the shoot proved to be a perfect California day with sunny blue skies and sheep-like puffy clouds. Jon's wife, Liesal, joined in using her hospitality and organizational gifts.

Since this was the last day of shooting, all of us were well aware of the time constraints. Around 5:30 in the late afternoon, the DP (director of photography) was shooting a crucial scene at the bottom of a cliff. I could easily watch while standing under a canopy.

In this final scene, a large rock had to be repeatedly thrown down from the high cliff as the three main characters interacted below. Jon had rented a large fake rock and wanted to be sure it did not get broken, so one of the crew lay on the ground between the actors, deftly catching it over and over again.

At one point there was a disagreement regarding which shot angles were essential. I could sense tension on the team as they are losing light quickly. The DP pressed on, affirming to Jon that he could still make it work. At last all the necessary shots were completed. We all celebrated.

As the sun set, I felt it would be best for Jon to concentrate on his final wrap-up with his crew. As I drove off, looking in my rearview mirror, I felt both satisfying joy and a bit melancholy. Perhaps it was because this fun fantasy film distraction had ended, and now in contrast, I was heading down the mountain and back to reality.

Despite my sadness, I felt grateful that I happened to be in California getting my face treated so that I could witness Jonathan's work. The past three days were a gift—a refreshing highlight that brought light and life to my routine that had seemed so colorless and regimented for so long.

⚭

After a few more facial treatments, I flew back to Texas to be home with Tom. However, watching my face closely, Tom and I both decided it would be necessary to return to California in March for another three weeks of treatments. A lot more healing was still needed. This time I stayed with long time friends who happened to live close to Dr. Simpson's office. The bedroom they provided for me was lovely and quiet and decorated with a brightly colored pink and perky green surfing motif.

Dr. Simpson was encouraged with my healing progress. It was clear now that my face would be scarred in places and damaged for life, but the redness had substantially subsided.

During this second stint in California, I missed Tom and my family more than ever. So I was thrilled when Tom called one evening and said, "I'm flying out to be with you.

And Leaza wants to come too." A few days later, I found out that our son Steve was also joining us. Easter weekend was going to be fun.

Little did we all know that Jon and Liesal made plans for us to experience a quintessential southern California day.

⌒

As soon as Tom, Leaza and Steve flew into Burbank, Jon and Liesal took us all to a lovely restaurant in the hills above Pasadena. We enjoyed a tasty Mediterranean lunch looking out to the California hills. Then we drove to Grauman's Chinese Theatre, where we saw the Hollywood walk of fame and street actors dressed up as Marilyn Monroe and Johnny Depp as Captain Jack Sparrow from *Pirates of the Caribbean*. After we ate dessert at a local Hollywood spot, Jon and Liesal drove us up Mulholland Drive, which is known for being home to many rich and famous Hollywood elite over the years.

The fun continued. That evening, we all met up with about forty of Jon and Liesal's friends at a Mexican restaurant. Most were fellow creatives, directors, writers, and actors. The young, energetic crowd filled up most of the room. It was easy to see that they were well-connected, trying to survive and make it in the Hollywood entertainment industry and wanting to make a difference with their gifts and their lives. I laughed with delight to myself as a mariachi band began to play. The musicians were dressed in matching white outfits accented with gold fringe. *This couldn't be any more California.*

After dinner everyone drove to a nearby apartment complex. Entering the front entrance we gathered in the open courtyard surrounded on all sides by two-story apartments. A couple of the guys laboriously carried a giant flat-screen TV downstairs and placed it onto a table. Our group expanded as some of Steve's friends who had moved to California joined us. One of the young women was celebrating her birthday, so there was cake, ice cream, and drinks, all adding fun and flare to the festivities.

At last, with great anticipation we all gathered in lawn chairs as Jon and his fellow crew set up to reveal for the very first time their short film. I couldn't believe that I not only had the chance to see the scenes being shot, but also now I could see the very first showing. Back in January I also had heard some of the original soundtrack by the gifted composer they had hired. Now I could experience everything put together.

Jon spoke on behalf of the production team, "Thanks for coming out to our premiere. We hope you enjoy it. We've named our short film simply, *The Wheel.* You will soon see why."

The plot was based around three escapees who had all been locked up together to a wagon wheel while being "taken in" by two bounty hunters. Somehow they had escaped the wagon but were still chained to the wheel as they were being chased through the rocky hills. It was a blast to hear everyone break out in laughter during the hilarious scenes. Afterward, we all clapped and congratulated the film team.

What a lovely, balmy, absolutely memorable California evening—experiencing the joy of watching a good film with family, good friends, and good food. It was surprising to me that my face repair had taken me all the way to southern California, to a place of joy and restoration.

As a side note, Jon called a few weeks later. "Our short film did make it into the top contenders in the annual Indie film festival so it will be shown to a larger audience in a theatre." Awesome.

Chapter 35

ॐ

"Mom Needs Me"

Loneliness set in after Tom, Steve, and Leaza all left, but I had to remain in California to complete my treatments. As the three weeks of treatments continued, one morning Dr. Simpson showed me photos of my face. "See, this is how your face looked when you first arrived in January. Here are your most recent photos. Can you see how your skin color is far less red and notice how the texture looks so much smoother and healthier?"

"Yes, I can. There's such a marked difference. I can't believe it. Thanks for all you've done!"

When I got home that afternoon, I received an urgent call from my sister Lauri. "Can you please come to Seattle? I need help taking care of Mom." I had not realized that Lauri had taken medical leave from her job in order to provide Mom with daily care for the past few weeks.

I immediately flew out to Seattle to be with Lauri and Mom. My face would have to wait. I placed my trusty mask in my carry-on. It was my constant companion. I still wore it whenever I was indoors.

I could tell that Mom's health was deteriorating rapidly. During the first few days of my visit she had just enough energy to go up and down stairs to her bedroom. Knowing that I liked to organize, she asked me to help sort through her important medical and financial papers. She had stored them in large colorful plastic file bins lined up along a wall.

Mom's mind was sharp, recalling specific files, culling out important papers from different bins that she wanted her brother and sister-in-law to look at when they arrived the following week. With our teamwork, it wasn't difficult helping Mom organize her already very organized files.

A few days later, Mom decided she needed to move downstairs. While she spent most of the day lying on the long blue sofa, she seemed more fidgety and nervous. I wanted to share my deep love for her. I began, "Mom, I want you to know how much you mean to me . . ."

She stopped me. "No need to talk about that. I feel that God is going to heal me."

What could I say now? I felt disappointed that I was not allowed to tell her all that I wanted to convey—all that she meant to me, to share the wonderful ways she had blessed my life, and how deeply I appreciated her love. Yet, apparently she was not comfortable with me sharing how much I would miss her while she was focusing on living. I assumed she knew and that's what mattered.

✑

Later that week I asked Mom, "Would it be okay if I video-taped you as you talk about your family history and how you met Dad and stuff?"

"Sure," she said. So that afternoon I began recording. With fond reflection, Mom began to talk about her life as a child, her love of playing the piano, and how she and Dad met at the University of Wisconsin through a skit that her sorority and his fraternity did together.

Mom's breathing was labored as she lay propped up on the blue sofa, but she talked freely between breaths. I always loved hearing Mom tell about her personal discovery at age twenty-three that she was really good at something—teaching. I knew that she was not only an excellent teacher, but she absolutely loved it as a calling. I felt proud that she had positively influenced countless students throughout her lifetime, teaching practically every grade level from elementary through master's level.

I thought back to when Mom was writing her doctoral thesis while I was visiting one summer. She would always stop her work on her computer and give me her full attention whenever I wanted to talk. Somehow Mom always had a way of working hard, giving every project 110%, and also giving people priority at the same time.

Thankfully, the next day, Mom gave me permission to record some of the experiences in her and our family's spiritual life. As I videoed, she spoke with joy. "When I was in my early thirties, a friend asked me if I wanted to study the Bible with her in a small group. I had never studied the Bible, so it sounded interesting. Within three weeks I realized how little I knew about God, Jesus, and the Holy Spirit. I could grasp God the Father and Jesus the Son. But why the Spirit? One afternoon, while I was talking to God in the kitchen about my confusion, telling him, 'God, I don't know whether there is a Holy Spirit.' All of a sudden I felt a whoosh, as if I was flooded by God's presence coming down on me. As you know, I've never been a touchy-feely person, but then and there I asked Jesus to be my Savior, to forgive my sins. I knew God was real."

As I taped her, Mom continued to talk with animation in between heavy breaths. She explained how Dad, while on a business trip, heard Billy Graham speak in Madison Square Garden. He walked down the aisle to make a commitment to Christ. She also spoke of how her father prayed to receive Jesus just three days before he died at age 91, as her mom stood by his bed in the hospital. I realized that a spiritual legacy had spread in all directions from Mom and Dad. We three girls and many relatives also became followers of Jesus because of my parents' influence. Once again, I felt blessed to record from Mom's heart and with Mom's voice her spiritual journey and the lasting and ongoing legacy for our family. We would now have a record, a permanent memory of her special and purposeful life.

∽

By the time my uncle and aunt came a week or so later, Mom's energy level had markedly deteriorated. She rested on the sofa downstairs most of the day. Yet it seemed that just their presence with us for four days buoyed her spirits. My aunt, being particularly gifted with accounting, was able to go through all of her files and papers to see whether a few still needed to be addressed. We then took Mom to the bank to get some documents signed and notarized. Afterward Mom said, "Now, I can finally relax."

Adding to our group, my sister Kari flew in from California. That same evening, my aunt gathered us three girls in the family room. "I have done hospice care in a variety of settings, so I wanted you to know that you don't need to be afraid when your mom's time is near."

We asked her what we should expect.

"You know that passage in Isaiah that speaks of 'running and not being weary and walking and not fainting'? I think those truths reflect our lives when we enter heaven. We will no longer be confined to our human limitations when we are with God. We will finally be able to run and not be weary, and walk and not faint." She answered all our questions about the death process and comforted our hurting hearts.

The following morning we took Mom to see her family doctor, a wonderful man with a heart of gold. After some medical evaluations, he told her that he guessed that she would have at the most a week to a month to live.

Mom looked absolutely crushed. We all felt crushed along with her.

That afternoon Mom asked me to drive her to see Dad at his group home. When we arrived, Dad was already sitting on the left side of a long brown leather sofa in the sunny family room, waiting for Mom to come in. She sat down next to him, grabbed his hand, and leaned her head on his right shoulder. Tears filled her eyes. She sat there very still for a long time. She did not tell Dad that her end was nearing quickly.

When she got up, she kissed Dad's cheek. "I love you, John."

As I helped her into Lauri's van, she spoke. "That is the last time I will go and visit your father." She added, "I don't have the energy to do it anymore." I felt like weeping right then and there, but I held back my tears. This was my mom's time to grieve.

Chapter 36

He Gives and Takes Away

Our daughter Leaza, now graduated from college, called once she heard the news about Mom. "I have permission to cut short my internship with the PR firm. I am flying out in two days."

I eagerly looked forward to her arrival. Leaza has a wonderful gift of mercy and helps, and I knew she wanted to help her Gram very much. So Leaza, Lauri, and I became the mighty trio. We took on various roles in caring for Mom—talking with hospice and nursing staff, preparing meals, and helping her with the most basic of tasks.

It often rains and is overcast in Seattle. While looking out of the windows of Lauri's home as the drizzling rain came down, I thought about how much it reflected our sadness. Every evening, Mom wanted us to read to her parts from the book *Heaven,* by Randy Alcorn. She knew she was heading there soon and wanted to hear what heaven might be like.

Meanwhile, I continued maintaining my facial regimen with specialty creams while faithfully wearing my face mask the entire day, even when nurses and Lauri's friends dropped by. One afternoon, as we all sat at the kitchen table one of the visiting nurses said, "You actually look quite young with your face pressed into the plastic." *Her compliment was so encouraging to hear. If she only knew how far my face had come.*

∼

I became concerned about how Dad must be feeling. Mom had visited him almost every day for the past thirteen years while he resided in various caregiving homes. Now she could not. Surely Dad felt the loss. Although Lauri's family, Leaza and I were visiting Dad a lot, it wasn't the same.

"Let's get Dad over to see Mom," someone suggested. We talked with Dad's wonderful caretakers and they agreed to bring Dad over the following Saturday afternoon.

Mom wanted to look special for Dad. I cannot remember a day when she did not look nice for him, with her hair and makeup always in place. She wanted to do the same again. My sister found a hairdresser willing to come to the house to do Mom's hair. The stylist did a great job and Mom looked beautiful.

It was a great feat for the staff to get my stiff dad into their car, and then to maneuver him out of it into a wheelchair. It took four of us to haul him up the small flight of stairs and onto the front porch of Lauri's home—but it was all worth the effort.

At last Dad was rolled into the foyer. He held a huge bouquet of yellow roses on his lap, Mom's favorites. As we wheeled him into the room where Mom waited, they both almost burst into tears, seeing one another again. But they controlled their emotions, looking instead as if they were grieving deeply inside. We placed Dad's wheelchair next to Mom, who sat on the sofa, propped up by pillows, and they held hands quietly.

We Skyped Jon and Liesal in California because they wanted to join in the occasion, despite the distance. It was very difficult for us to hold it together. Liesal, in tears, had to leave her place in front of the screen.

After about forty-five minutes we wheeled Dad back out to the car. I held onto his hands as he sat in the front seat. His hands shook with emotion as he looked up at me. He did not cry any tears. His Parkinson's disease restricted his chest movements, but I could tell he was devastated to see his beloved wife, Barb, visibly worsening. He was crying inside.

⁓

I took the following week off and flew back home to be with Tom in Texas while Leaza remained with Mom. She was soon accompanied by her brother Jonathan for extra physical and emotional support. After I returned to Seattle, Leaza went back home to Dallas.

I found Mom to be in the last stage of her life. Even with the strong pain meds, just the slightest of movements would cause her to cry out in excruciating pain. Her doctor came by and upped her morphine so she would no longer suffer. Mom finally slept soundly. I held her hands, as that always seemed to relax her.

Scott, who had just finished his freshman year of college, flew out the next day to say his last goodbyes to Gram. I was grateful for his company.

The night of his arrival, I sat chatting with a night caregiver in the family room. Mom's rapid and labored breathing suddenly slowed down. We looked at one another, and together, we went over to check her out closely. She was now in a coma. Her hands no longer responded to mine, but I was so grateful that she was now fully relieved of her pain.

As I slept fitfully upstairs that night, I felt afraid Mom might pass while I tried to sleep. The caregiver, however, reassured me she would awaken me if needed.

I woke up early in the morning and found that Mom was still alive. Her dear dog, Benji, a black and white Shih Tzu, had been placed at the bottom of her bed. He snuggled next to her feet as if he wanted to be extra close. Worship music was playing in the background.

Throughout the morning Lauri and her daughter Jennifer, along with Scott and I, each took turns talking to Mom, sharing some of her favorite Bible verses. We also sang to her.

As I sensed Mom's body fading, Scott and I held her hands, he on the left and I on the right. Together we sang the song, "Blessed Be Your Name." Just as we sang about God and how "He gives and takes away" (magnificent words from the book of Job), Mom just stopped breathing as if the key to her engine had been turned off. Silence. I knew her soul had left this world. I had felt tearful all morning, but now I cried.

I was so grateful to be with Mom on her last day on this earth, and that Scott and I were together holding her hands as she left us and our world to join our Father in heaven. As my aunt had told us it would be, it was a blessing and a privilege to be there when my mom took her last breath.

How appropriate and timely it seemed to have been singing, "He gives and takes away . . . Blessed be his name," just as Mom was taken away into heaven.

My sister's son, Daniel, soon arrived. All five of us surrounded my mom, holding hands, and one by one we thanked God for her life. We all cried. I cried knowing that I would never see her alive and speak to her again in this world. I knew she was in glorious heaven and was seeing amazing things. Yet we felt such deep sadness.

I wept as I sat in the family room while the funeral staff took Mom's body away. "Oh, Mama," I cried, "I'm going to miss you so much." Life, as I knew it had forever changed.

⌒

Cousins, aunts and uncles, grandchildren, and many friends came in from all over to be part of Mom's memorial service. It is remarkable how the death of a loved one can become a reunion of shared love.

As we gathered at Mom's church, some of our family friends came over to ask how I was doing. "Your face is really looking good. We've been so concerned for you and have prayed for you over the past months." I thanked them and was once again reminded of how blessed I was to have people really care for me from far away places, and also see how well my face was doing.

⌒⌒

Being a joyous, upbeat person, Dad always had a way of making people laugh. Mom's memorial service would be no different. As the pastor was talking about Mom's life from the front, we heard a couple of grunts coming from the left. We all looked over to see Dad fast asleep and making himself known. His head drooped on his chest due to his Parkinson's, and he slept soundly. Kari, Lauri, and I tried to wake him up. Once awake, he would only stay awake for a few minutes. Occasionally he would grunt and all of us would laugh again. Dad's humanity added some much-needed levity to the final celebration of Mom's life.

Chapter 37

⁒

Wrestling in the Clouds

I returned home to the Dallas area in mid-May, fourteen months after my ordeal began. I wore the mask only occasionally now, for my face had basically stabilized. As the summer wore on, I found myself grieving the loss of my mom as well as the loss of my face. I needed a place to process it all. Tom suggested a counselor, Jan Fleming, who he had met through work. I made an appointment.

As soon as I entered the counselor's office I felt at home. Her cozy office was located high up in the tall building so I could look out to the skies. Jan greeted me and together we began to talk.

"Jan, I have had a year and a half that has seemed so hard . . . "

Jan listened well. Her kind words and wise advice helped me move forward. We met on and off for the next year. One afternoon, she surprised me with an observation.

"Kristi, you should be commended. Did you know that many people who go through an extreme time of trial like yours sometimes become involved with an addiction or another harmful coping mechanism? You never did that."

She's right. Hey—that is good. And it did make sense that when encountering pain we often want to avoid it or soften its crushing pressure by covering it with an addiction of some sort.

I don't know why I never did something detrimental to myself while my face was a mess. I think it helped that I had a strong family and had been supported by so many friends throughout my time of trial. Most importantly, I also had a perspective that God was watching me throughout all that had happened in my life. I knew that he never promised people that they wouldn't suffer. Life is full of both easy and hard times, and this was one of mine.

ↄ

During another session I wanted to talk with Jan specifically about my honest wrestling with God. "You know, as I have studied Job, throughout the book he complained to God a lot for not defending him to his friends. He was fully honest with God with how he felt. I'm the same way. "I'm always telling God how I feel, and ask him many questions, especially when I don't understand why something tragic happened. That's okay, isn't it?"

"Kristi, did you know that God often reveals more of himself to the wrestlers? Those who wrestle with God are conversing with him, begging for help, expressing their raw feelings. And think about it, God often comes back to them and explains new truth. Consider Moses, David, Abraham, and also Job. They questioned and argued with God. In response, he spoke to them and revealed more of himself to each of them as they wrestled with him. I actually think most of us need to wrestle with God more than we do."

So my wrestlings and others' wrestlings were not only acceptable, but God was listening and willing to converse. As he was responding, he wanted to reveal more of himself to me and other wrestlers, just like he did with Job. Such a profound concept.

⌒

Although I no longer needed to wear my plastic face mask, I did try to keep my face out of the sun as much as possible. I often wore wide brimmed hats. When I drove, especially on sunny days, I either held up something like a magazine at the left side of my face or I wore my aqua-colored face covering connected to my sunglasses. Sometimes I forgot that wearing my sunglass face protection in public would scare people.

One lunchtime in late August, I was invited to meet up with Tom and the office staff at a local sandwich shop. Being a boiling hot and sunny Texas day, I put on my head band and the sunglasses with the material sewn on to protect my face.

Just as I pulled up to the curb of the restaurant, I saw one of Tom's coworkers, Dave Trent, standing there gazing off in the distance. All of a sudden he noticed me through the front windshield. He jumped back, his face showing it all—utter shock and fear. His eyes blew up as big as frisbees. Realizing that I had literally terrorized the poor man with my face covering, I yanked off my sun glasses, opened the car door, and jumped out, saying, "It's me. It's me. I'm so sorry." He put his hand over his chest and said, "Thank goodness." I found out at lunch that he had worked for NYPD and his daughter had been in one of the Twin Towers when the terrorist attacks took place on 9/11. His daughter ran out to safety after he called her and warned her to leave the building as quickly as possible.

I decided that day would be the last time I would wear my "terrorist" look in public.

Chapter 38

Chapter 38

Beautiful Scars

One afternoon as Tom was driving, I asked him a question I recently had been wondering about. "Tom, do you prefer the way my face looked before I had the laser procedure done, with all my deep lines and wrinkles, or do your prefer me now, looking a bit younger, but with my face discoloration and scarring?

He answered, "It's a toss-up."

"Hah, hah! That's not the right answer. You're supposed to say that you like my face so much better now. I can't go back to how it was before."

We both had a good laugh.

I know that many people prayed that I would not scar, and I so appreciated their tender desires on my behalf. Thankfully,

I scarred only minimally. But my skin is a wreck. It's paper thin, and without makeup, you can see the hypopigmentation (missing skin color where the melanin has been wiped out) alongside blotchy red and purple areas.

Most people think I look pretty normal when I wear makeup. However, I can still cause those who don't know my story to be shocked. Two years to the day after my facial laser procedure on March 8, I awoke from a dead sleep when I heard our dog barking as he began to run out of our bedroom. Wanting to keep him in, I rushed toward the French doors, hoping to stop his escape. Somehow my left foot got stuck between the doors and a huge box of stored items we needed to put up in the attic. I was catapulted into the air, and then fell on my left side with a nasty thud on the bedroom floor. I cried out, "I'm hurt! I've broken something!"

Tom called 911. After I was taken to the hospital by ambulance, X-rays indicated I had broken my left femur. I woke up from surgery to see three medical staff staring down at me. One of the women tentatively said, "Your face looks purple and red. We are concerned about its circulation and damage. Is there something we should know?"

I laughed as I pointed to my face. "Don't worry. This is how I always look now. That's a whole other story. Can you up the morphine?" They seemed quite relieved.

Is there value in wounds, in scars? Years ago, while in grad school, one of my professors told the story of how she broke her clavicle when she fell down some stairs. "I often wore a scarf to cover up my scar. One day, one of the women attending my classes who was from Africa politely spoke to me after one of the sessions. 'Professor, perhaps you shouldn't try to cover your scar. In my country scars are a sign of great honor. Scars show we've been through a war and we are still alive.'"

Each of us carry scars. They may be physical or emotional scars. They may be relational. Our scars can be honored as items of profound beauty, not aesthetically, but on the deepest heart, soul, and personal level. Our scars remind us that we have been wounded and are still here living and moving forward.

As I look at my facial scars, I'm grateful that my face recovered as well as it did. I've also thought about Job's scars. During the time when I had no answers regarding my face, a friend of mine, Allie, showed me her wrist. "Look, see these two scars? A few years ago, I got two boils here, and had to have an infusion of antibiotics to get rid of them. I also had to take prescription pain meds to cope because the pain was so excruciating."

It does seem logical that most likely Job bore many scars after his body finally recovered. He would carry them the remainder of his life, a reminder of his terrible, boil-infested trial and severe loss. Yet those scars would also become a public witness to Job's courageous loyalty to God when so much had been taken away.

And Job's scars would also testify to God's faithfulness to mercifully and generously restore to Job what had been lost. Thankfully, after his severe losses, Job and his wife were given ten more children to love. Additionally, his new wealth, businesses, and influence enabled him to once again become a vital part of his community. He would continue to make a positive difference in his world, scars and all.

ᴄ⌐

Our Lord Jesus, too, is known by his scars. After his crucifixion and resurrection, he appeared to his disciples and then to more than five hundred others in his bodily form, with visible scars on his hands, feet, and side. Jesus' scars proclaim the depth of his wounds—suffering to the fullest extent as he gave his life in our behalf. He lovingly saved us by being impaled on a tree.

Jesus' scars also reflect the magnificence of his resurrection. Even today we hear numerous stories of Jesus appearing to people around the world in visions and dreams. Some who have seen him say Jesus appears dressed in a white robe with scars on his hands and feet. And each of their lives are changed forever as they embrace the resurrected Jesus as their Savior.

There is a sacred beauty in scars.

Chapter 39

Simple Prayers and Complexity

My prayers throughout all the many months of my facial trial were not elaborate or dramatic like Job's rich, figurative language. I am forever grateful for God's answer to my most often repeated and simple prayer sometimes spoken in utter desperation, "God, please help me."

Throughout the long months I longed for someone out of the blue to come up to me and say, "I know what is wrong with your face and I have the answer." Alas, that never happened. Someone told me that the verse about "seek and you shall find" can encourage us to take action as we pray. God helps us find answers as we seek options in different directions. And God works as we go out and knock.

While praying throughout my facial trial, I actively sought help in many directions. It wasn't until my discovery of a wise and caring nurse that my suffering would find a permanent solution. How I would have preferred skipping the many months of searching and knocking when the medical experts didn't know how to solve the problem of my infected and wounded face. Thankfully, my seeking at last found an answer.

But, we know that is not always the case. Undoubtedly, some of you reading this story are currently enduring severe suffering that has not gone away. Perhaps, you have been yearning and praying, seeking relief for days, months, and even years.

I have come to realize that the complexity of pain and suffering in relation to how God works is incomprehensible. We all seek answers, but trying to understand God in the midst of pain and suffering—that will always be a place of mystery. Why does God heal, restore, bring peace to a situation, while many are not healed, restored, and live in turmoil? I was fortunate to get my health back. Job was fortunate to eventually get what he had lost in many ways. But that is not how life always works out. We often don't get the story-book ending.

How do we relate to God who cannot be put into a box? Have you noticed? He seems to never work the same way twice, and often not as we expect. Like Job, don't we all long for him to intervene exactly as seems best as we plead and beg? But he doesn't always do that. Job's story is also different from anyone else's. In each of our life stories, God at times is working in ways that we can't see and in ways incomprehensible.

When we find God's ways confusing, we, like Job, are free to tell him how we feel. In the midst of his severe loss, Job implored God with fervor and passion, "God can't you stand up for me against my cruel friends? I beg of you."

I often talk to God, when I hear of suffering that happened to others. "That horrific tragedy doesn't make any sense." Or, "God, you could have stopped that disaster. I don't understand why you didn't, or how you work the way you do." Perhaps you too have prayed, "God, I feel so discouraged because I've prayed so long and hard and yet the disturbing situation only seems to get worse."

We yearn for something beyond the brokenness of this world as we ask God to help us understand his ways.

After many months of Job pleading his case, God himself would respond to him in a blustery storm and ask him, "Job, where were you when I made the seas, the mountains, and set the natural world into motion?" Basically he was asking Job, as the winds flew around him, "Can you make the world go round?" Then Job answered the Lord in the end and said,

"I know that You can do all things,
And that no purpose of Yours can be thwarted.
'Who is this that hides counsel without knowledge?'
Therefore I have declared that which I did not understand,

Things too wonderful for me, which I
did not know."

'Hear, now, and I will speak;

I will ask You, and You instruct me.'

"I have heard of You by the hearing of
the ear;

But now my eye sees You;

Therefore I retract,

And I repent in dust and ashes."

Can we picture Job face down saying, "I repent. I finally see you, God, in ways I didn't before. I really don't know anything."

My heart goes out to you who are suffering now. I wish there was a sure cure, a beautiful solution for your physical, relational, and emotional woundings. Some of you will be healed and your brokenness will be mended. Some of you will find restoration. However, for those of you who are suffering and grieving today and for those of you whose loved ones are hurting, may you be comforted as your reach toward God.

Your excruciating pain, your devastating trial, your extreme loss is both profane and sacred.

Chapter 40

꙰

Dancing

Job is known today for his heroic patience and endurance under monumental trials. Understandably, even as his life became fully restored, Job would at times think back and miss all that he had lost during his time of severe loss—his seven sons and three daughters, his servants, his livestock. But now that it was all over and he was on the other side, surely it was a time to dance.

Can't we imagine him rejoicing with his family and friends at dinner? "My boils are all gone! I have no more pain! I can't believe it! Please pass the lamb kabobs." Can we hear him gleefully shouting over the next few years, "I have a new baby boy! I have a new baby girl!" Can't we hear him share with his friends? "Isn't it wonderful today? We were able to rescue the widow and six orphans from danger. The poor little ones had hardly any clothing. And just last week we were able to provide food and shelter for the

weary travelers from the West." Can we picture him dancing as he celebrates with his entire community, "Wow, can
you believe how God has multiplied the livestock this year
again? We'll need to build even more pens and hire more
workers, and get more dogs to shepherd the flocks." And as
Job goes to bed with his wife he celebrates, "This evening
Abidah and our caravan came back safely. I can't wait to
smell the spices. Did you hear about the beautiful pearls
and crystals?"

&

Likewise, I will also rejoice in present days. Today my face,
like Job's scarred body, is a living testament of dark days
and God's grace. As I look back at the photos of my infected
face, I sometimes wonder how I kept my sanity. Surely it
was God. I also realize that the staph infection eventually
could have ended my life had I not found a solution.

Today I rejoice that I am blessed to be alive, and to
love and to be loved. Just as Job surely danced once again,
now is my time for dancing.

&

On Sunday mornings, our son Jon and his wife, Liesal, have
regularly volunteered at their church in Pasadena to watch
handicapped children, many on the autism spectrum,. As
part of "In His Image Ministries," not only have they
blessed the children but have given the often stressed-out
parents a much-needed break.

Jon wrote something for one of their celebrations that spoke to me deeply.

> "We've learned that God's kingdom looks like an imperfect world, where suffering exists right next to God's sovereignty and love. We still don't understand why things are the way they are. What we do know is that at the end of this crazy life, there is a friend waiting for us who will wipe every tear from our eyes and transform all our suffering into inexplicable joy."

Postscript

When people hear my story, one of the most often asked question is, "Did you consider suing the original doctor for his part in causing your face to have a major medical problem?"

The answer is yes.

Tom and I contacted a few malpractice lawyers in the Dallas-Fort Worth metroplex. The legal staff at each office were very interested in my case, but they soon realized that it would be a long shot. Apart from seeing the disaster of my face, it would be hard to prove gross negligence, especially in the state of Texas. Sadly, a few years prior to my facial disaster, insurance companies persuaded the state legislature to implement strict malpractice laws. And due to the tort reform very few lawyers now deal with malpractice in Texas.

In the end I realized that my primary doctors believed my case would be difficult to prove, and they did not want to be involved with a stressful lawsuit. Neither did I.

However, my doctors in California told me that had I lived there I would have received compensation to cover my expenses along with payments for my pain and suffering and the lifetime damage to my face. I did report the doctor to a medical board, and for two years they kept the case open. One day, I received a final letter noting that the board would not go forward with any legal action. I teared up a bit. It was another reminder of my traumatic experience. And another end. I was glad that this chapter of my life had closed.

We three girls:
I, Lauri, and Kari

Kari, Lauri, and I

Middle of three sisters

My face on day of
initial procedure

Concerned
at home that
something
is wrong

Awake at night,
waiting to call
a new doctor

Tom and I with our
children when we
lived in Budapest

Photo of Tom and me used
for our newsletter
"But I am smiling."

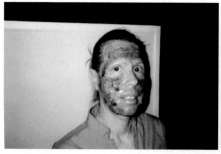

Waiting for the crusting to fall off

Tray of caring letters, cards, and messages

My face when the infection was coming back

My Diary

My sister's dogs

My face in June

My face in July

My face in August

August 20th,
before I began
wound care
treatment

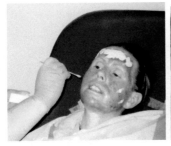 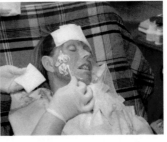

Treatment by Jenny,
the wound care nurse

August 24, 3rd day of
treatment by Jenny

My friend,
"Monkey"

Our coffee table
being used
for treatment

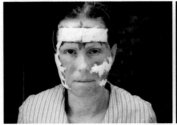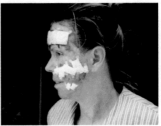

When the skin on my forehead had to be removed

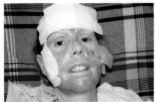

Treatment of my
full face, section
by section

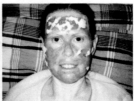

My face is
recovering well.

Tom and I at Dr. Joy's
office, excited to show
my face healing

Jenny had just
completed my treatment
during the 2nd week.

Tom and I with our dog
Winston, thrilled that
my face now no longer
needs bandages

Tom's mom with me
in Pennsylvania

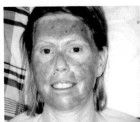

I now have intact skin!

Delighted
having a
new haircut
with Jenny

Dr. Joy and I
are encouraged
after starting the
treatments to
lessen the redness.

The watercolor that Tom and
I gave to Jenny as a gift

Prepared to go out with Mom, with and
without my protective gear

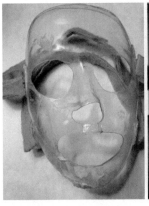 

My face mask from
the burn center

Face recovering well
with dermatologist, Dr.
Simpson in California

On the set of the
California film shoot

My Dad and I at Christmas

Scott with me on the day
Mom died with her dog, Benji

Tom and I with my
Dad on the day of
Mom's viewing

Leaza, Tom, with
me and my hat

Scott, Steve, Jonathan, and Leaza as teenagers

Our four children with their spouses and our grandchildren

Tom and I enjoying our grandkids

Epilogue

Suffering Job among friends dealing with
a loving God of the unexpected

Finding God in the Midst of Suffereing:
A glimpse into the life of Job and others

꒰ᴑ꒱

Throughout the writing process of this book I saved the manuscript on my computer under the name *My Face Book*. It would have made a great title, but I thought that I just might have some copyright issues. When a friend suggested, "Finding a Face" the title stuck—clear and simple.

As I wrote my story, a much longer second portion about pain and suffering, especially as it relates to the life of Job, also grew. When I tried to interweave what I was learning from Job into my face story, the topics bogged it down. Talking about such deep and heart-touching issues is heavy. And I did not want this book to become that.

So, instead of writing another book I have put all the topics regarding Job and suffering online for anyone to read and use. A list of some of the chapters follows this section and can be downloaded through the link: *www.kristimiller.org.*

This second part, which focuses on finding God in the midst of our suffering, is an offering for those who question God and yearn to know him more as he truly is. It's also for those willing to quit trying to stuff God into a constricted six-walled box. He doesn't fit. He has never chosen to fit into our human boxes.

God often works in ways that we find not only confusing at times, but aggravating, and even maddening.

As we look at the life of Job we realize that he suffered in nearly every way imaginable. And the level of his suffering is almost unimaginable. God had watched Job provide loving, intentional care for his family, his servants, and the most needy in his community. God considered Job to be the most blameless man on earth. Incredible. So, why did this honorable man get hit with so much tragedy?

Job's life illustrates that suffering doesn't come just to the bad or to those who are experiencing negative karma. God makes that clear. Although Job lived an exemplary life, he was the one who lost most everything—his children, his livelihood, and his health. We still see this incongruence every day. Can we provide a formula for why the little child gets cancer while the heinous dictator reigns for decades?

I had a friend whose mother was dying of lung cancer. Although the doctors and nurses at the hospital tried everything to mitigate her pain, nothing worked. She screamed out, bursting in tears and anguish, "I want to die. I want to die." There was no "peace that passes all understanding." No angels drifted down from heaven to comfort this woman. There was only pure unadulterated physical pain, "I cannot endure this." God chose not to intervene, even as her loved ones prayed and as she desperately begged.

What could we possibly say to this woman and her family about God and suffering? No quip, no quote, no assertion is adequate.

That's why we can identify with Job in some way. His personal story of extreme suffering has no-sugar-coating. Job kept it real. It is so hard to see at times, but studying Job showed me that God does deeply care about our suffering, but he doesn't always stop it. Like Job and countless others who love God, we cry out to God from the depths of our hearts and wrestle with him in the midst of our suffering.

We can see part of the backstory for Job's suffering. But one of my professors in grad school also noted that God does not reveal all that is going on when Job suffered. Only God knows the entire, huge, mind-blowing, and God-glorifying picture.

And the older I get, I've come to realize the questions I have still persist and deepen. We will not always know the answers. Can we tell God how we feel in our frustration, confusion, and even anger? He is listening just as he listened to Job's words long ago:

"I would present *my* case before Him
And fill my mouth with arguments ...

Behold, I go forward but He is not *there*,
And backward, but I cannot perceive Him ...

But He knows the way I take;
When He has tried me, I shall come forth as gold.
My foot has held fast to His path;
I have kept His way and not turned aside.
I have not departed from the command of His lips …

And *what* His soul desires, that He does …

When I consider, I am terrified of Him.
It is God *who* has made my heart faint,
And the Almighty *who* has dismayed me,
But I am not silenced by the darkness,
Nor deep gloom *which* covers me." (Job 23:2–17).

Looking at pain and suffering through the heart and words of Job provided a place for me to grieve and find hope. As we each embark on our unique journeys of life and faith, we will discover that God embraces us in our times of relative peace as well as times of struggle, as we try to wrap our minds, emotions, and hearts around a God who does whatever he pleases. That is what Job declares.

⌒

Can we tell God exactly how we feel, even in our darkest thoughts, like Job so candidly spoke? Can we also hang on to him when life gives us or others a crushing blow? I call it "fingernail faith." Despite Job's many complaints and passionate pleadings, in the midst of God's silence, he refused to turn aside. He kept his feet firm, remaining loyal and devoted to God even while stuck in the midst of his severe losses and unsparing pain.

God would eventually respond.

Our faith in God expands in bigger, deeper ways as we become more willing, much like Job, to engage God more openly. It may seem far less comfortable to address God with our questions as to why or why not he does or doesn't do actions that make sense to us. But in the end wrestling with God is far more life giving to us and honoring to God. We become willing to throw out our human contrived boxes that don't fit a complex God. As we wrestle with and embrace our incomprehensible God as a mystery, we no longer sit contentedly with simplistic answers about who God is and how he works.

God is love. God is good. God is all knowing. God is all powerful. We will not always understand his will and ways. We know that his lovingkindness never ceases. His declaration of loyal love, his desire to comfort, his identification with our pain as he tenderly binds our wounds shows us that God is in the midst of our loss and pain.

I hope you will enjoy getting to know Job as a man who loved people deeply, was wounded cruelly, and never stopped reaching out toward God.

Topics regarding Job and Suffering
Visit www.kristimiller.org

Notes

A reminder: The names of people, their descriptions, and locations (except for my family) have been changed to provide anonymity and to keep the story central.

Note: Chicago style was used, therefore the ®, ©, and ™ marks are not indicated within the text body for references to goods, business names, services, musical, dramatic, literary and art works. They have been listed here in the notes.

Foreword
1. "God knows you to the deepest depths and loves you to the skies." Quote by Daniel Rangel from talk, "Sexuality and the Gospel: Where Do We Go From Here?" Austin Ridge Baptist Church, Austin, TX, September 31, 2018.

Chapter 2 The Incalculable Riches of Crazy Days, the back story to my story
Airhead® Wendy's® NBA®

Chapter 5 Investigation
Botox®

Chapter 10 Helmet Face
Taco Delight® Jamba Juice®

Chapter 11 I Matter
Victoria's Secret®

Chapter 14 It's Baaack . . .
A Few Good Men © *1992,* director Rob Reiner, production company Castle Rock Entertainment, Warner Brothers, Beverly Hills.

Chapter 16 Job: Beginning of a Long-Term Friendship
"The Lord gives and takes away" from"The Lord gave and the Lord has taken away. Blessed be the name of the Lord" (Job 1:21 NASB).

Chapter 19 Small Excursions and Sorry Comforters
Lyrics for Cares Chorus can be found at "Cares Chorus" © *1978,* Kelly Willard, Universal Music, Brentwood Benson Publishing Admin. by Brentwood-Benson Music Publishing, Inc., Brentwood,TN.

"Bless the Lord, O my soul, and all that is within me, bless His holy name" (Psalm 103:1 NASB).

"Like one who takes off a garment on a cold day, or like vinegar on soda, is he who sings songs to a troubled heart" (Proverbs 25:20 NASB).

The phrase, "without cause" from Job 2:3 NASB.

"The Lord said to Satan, 'Have you considered My servant Job? For there is no one like him on the earth, a blameless and upright man fearing God and turning away from evil. And he still holds fast his integrity, although you incited Me against him to ruin him without cause'" (Job 2:3 NASB). So, Job, was actually suffering "without cause" for months, and was still remaining faithful to God.

"Therefore my harp is turned to mourning and my flute to the sound of those who weep" (Job 30:31 NASB).

"I will be like refined gold," (Job 23:10 NASB).

"Sorry comforters" from: "I have heard many such things; Sorry comforters are you all" (Job 16:2 NASB).

God declared twice that he was the most righteous man on earth. "But He knows the way I take; *When* He has tried me, I shall come forth as gold" (Job 23:10 NASB).

"It came about after the Lord had spoken these words to Job, that the Lord said to Eliphaz the Temanite, 'My wrath is kindled against you and against your two friends, because you have not spoken of Me what is right as My servant Job has'" (Job 42:7 NASB).

"Now therefore, take for yourselves seven bulls and seven rams, and go to My servant Job, and offer up a burnt offering for yourselves, and My servant Job will pray for you. For I will accept him so that I may not do with you *according to your* folly, because you have not spoken of Me what is right, as My servant Job has" (Job 42:8 NASB).

Only seven bulls and seven rams would suffice. See Job 42:8-9.

Chapter 20 Burn Doctor
ZYVOX®

Chapter 21 Fateful Decision
The Tonight Show with Jay Leno ©, production by NBC Studios, among many others, Burbank, CA, 1992-2014.
ZYVOX®

Chapter 22 "Where Are You in My Darkness?"
ZYVOX®
Poem: "Was That You Lord?" (After the death of a son) Kris Lamp, 1985.

Chapter 23 Top Doc, and a Scary Face
ZYVOX®

Chapter 24 With a Potato Chip Face, I Began to Wonder . . .
ZYVOX®
ER©, TV show. Produced by Constant c Productions and Amblin Television, in association with Warner Bros. Television, 1994-2009.

Chapter 25 "Don't Come Back"
ZYVOX® Silvadene®

Chapter 26 "I Know What to Do"
Q-tips® The Body Shop®

Chapter 27 A Healer
"The eensy weensy spider" went up the water spout or the " incy wincy spider" or "itsy bitsy spider." Written and known in various forms after 1920, it first appears as a nursery rhyme in 1948

in the American Folk Songs for Children a collection by Mike and Peggy Seeger.

Chapter 28 Wounding Wounds
Dillards® The Body Shop® McDonalds®

Chapter 29 A New Me
Artwork: "Evening Respite," watercolor by Kristi Miller, © 2003. (Inspired and painted from a photograph by John Lewis Stage (used by permission), The Birth of America, Grosset & Dunlap, NY, 1975.)

Chapter 30 Plastic Face
Velcro® NBA®

Chapter 31 Christmas
The Sound of Music © 1965, director and producer, Rob Weise, 20th Century Fox Studios, Los Angeles.

Tillamook Cheese Factory® or Tillamook Creamery®

Chapter 32 California, Here I Come
Mustang® Omnilux®

Chapter 33 Mom and I, and TV Time
Target® Omnilux®

The Assassination of Jesse James by the Coward Robert Ford © 2007, director Andrew Dominik, producers Warner Bros. and Ridley Scott's company, Scott Free

"Tis So Sweet to Trust in Jesus," first published in 1882, text by Luisa M. R. Stead and melody by William J. Kirkpatrick

Chapter 34 Film Crew—Fun Diversion
Hollywood Burbank Airport, legally named Bob Hope Airport®

Grauman's Chinese Theatre ©

Pirates of the Caribbean: The Curse of the Black Pearl is a 2003 ©, produced by Walt Disney Pictures and Jerry Bruckheimer, Burbank.

The Wheel © 2008, produced by Bob Oei, Patrick Shen and Jonathan Miller. Directed by Jonathan Miller, Patrick Shen. Written by Bob Oei.

Chapter 36 He Gives and Takes Away
Madison Square Garden®
Heaven © by Randy Alcorn, Tyndale House, Carol Stream, Il, 2004. Skype ®

"Blessed Be Your Name" Matt Redman and Beth Redman 2002, from the 2002 album *Where Angels Fear to Tread*, producer *Nathan Nockels.*

"Blessed be the God and Father of our Lord Jesus Christ, the Father of mercies and God of all comfort, who comforts us in all our affliction so that we will be able to comfort those who are in any affliction with the comfort with which we ourselves are comforted by God" (2 Corin- thians 1:3-4 NASB). NYPD®

Chapter 39 Simple Prayers and Complexity
"Seek and you shall find" from Matthew 7:7-8. Ask, and it will be given to you; seek, and you will find; knock, and it will be opened to you. For everyone who asks receives, and he who seeks finds, and to him who knocks it will be opened" (Matthew 7:7-8 NASB).

God himself would speak to him in a blustery storm in Job 38-42.

"I know that You can do all things ...Therefore I have declared that which I did not understand ...I repent ..." See Job 42:1-6 NASB.

"Our physical maladies, our deep sufferings are both profane and sacred," from comments made by Jim Neathery, who has dealt with palsy for decades.

Chapter 40 Dancing
Job's bounty returns in Job chapter 42.

"We've learned that God's kingdom looks like an imperfect world, where suffering exists right next to God's sovereignty and love. We still don't understand why things are the way they are. What we do know is that at the end of this crazy life, there is a friend waiting for us who will wipe every tear from our eyes and transform all our suffering into inexplicable joy."

Jonathan Miller, for "In His Image Ministries," Pasadena, 2008.